TAPESTRY

Collected Writings

*For Barbara,
Best wishes, always,
Pat Mote*

Patricia Mote

AuthorHouse™
1663 Liberty Drive
Bloomington, IN 47403
www.authorhouse.com
Phone: 1-800-839-8640

© *2010 Patricia Mote. All rights reserved.*

No part of this book may be reproduced, stored in a retrieval system, or transmitted by any means without the written permission of the author.

First published by AuthorHouse 2/3/2010

ISBN: 978-1-4490-5808-1 (sc)

Printed in the United States of America
Bloomington, Indiana

This book is printed on acid-free paper.

DEDICATION

To the newest members of our family at the time of this writing, my great-granddaughters, Hallie Suzanne and Aubree Grace

ACKNOWLEDGMENTS

My thanks and indebtedness—

To my daughter, Susan Lee, whose creative images grace these pages and lend depth to my thoughts;

To my capable, insightful assistants, Tammy Sanderell and Betsy Hinton;

To the editors who have improved upon and published some of these pieces;

To family members—especially my daughter, Pamela Weinantz, and my son, John Dietsch, my stepdaughters, Susan and Leslie Mote, and my stepson, Ralph Mote; my brother Joe McDonald and sister-in-law, Nancy—all of them for their love and encouragement through the years;

To my grandchildren—Brian, Jessica, Emily, Jennifer, Benjamin, Leana, Latricia, and Hannah—who may learn things about their grandmother they never knew.

To the Center for Learning for use of the photo of Sr. Bernadette Vetter and to Hanover College for the photo of Dr. Dorothy S. Bucks;

To friends who have read and critiqued or heard of these selections and to the memory of all those whose names appear in this *Tapestry*.

CONTENTS

INTRODUCTION — xi

THE LIGHT TOUCH

Scales Of Justice — 3
A Saga Of Customer Service — 5
Please Don't Landscape My Plate — 9
For Services Rendered — 12

LOOKING INWARD

Jewels In My Crown — 19
    Miss Helenka Sagl — 20
    Miss Helen Lotz — 23
    Dr. Dorothy Bucks — 27
    Miss Euzetta Foster — 32
    Sr. Bernadette Vetter, H.M. — 35
Influence From Across The Aisle And Over The Decades — 40
Carpe Diem — 44
Smoothing Out The Wrinkles — 47
Streets Of Heaven — 51

A BACKWARD LOOK

The Voice Of The Thirties — 55
Old Clifty Inn Revisited — 61
December Afternoon — 78
Honors Day: 1968 — 81
Flags, Ribbons, And A Root Canal — 87
Pulse Of A Nation — 91
Travels With Roci — 96
One September Morning — 99

PERSONS I WISH I'D MET

"Everyone Ought To Have Been Born Poor." Dorothy Fuldheim 107
"Stand Your Ground!" Joseph E. McDonald 117
Captain Edward J. Kennedy: A Worthy Smalltown Citizen 128

INTRODUCTION

Singer-songwriter Carole King described her life as a tapestry to "feel and see" but one that is impossible to hold. Her view of life as "an everlasting vision" and "a wondrous, woven magic" is aptly stated.

This slim volume attempts, however, to hold some of the vivid pieces of the tapestry of my life, woven over the past six decades. Some are memorable events; others merely describe pet peeves or aggravations such as "Please Don't Landscape My Plate" and "Scales of Justice." Others, such as "December Afternoon" or "One September Morning," recount episodes of sheer terror. Fond memories of people and places important to my growing-up years appear in "Jewels in My Crown" and "Clifty Inn Revisited," among others. Moments of keen excitement or awareness emerge in "Pulse of a Nation" and "Streets of Heaven."

While most of the writings shared here are personal essays, I've also included three pieces of historical fiction in the final section, People I Wish I'd Known. These are persons I hope you'll enjoy meeting. My life has been made richer through researching their lives.

P.M.

Berea, Ohio

August 2009

PART ONE
THE LIGHT TOUCH

SCALES OF JUSTICE

This particular sun-washed morning started out so well. Once the rest of the family was out of the house, I waltzed into the half-bath with my coffee to put on my makeup and my mindset for work. I had a feeling this would be a special day.

Special, all right! As I flicked on the light, I didn't even feel the coffee plunging down the front of my robe, and my spine was a frozen poker. Stretched in front of the vanity lay a black snake at least three feet long.

Somehow I got back to the kitchen for more coffee. Surely, I'd imagined what I'd seen. No more reading *National Geographic* at bedtime, I vowed. This was a midwestern suburb, not a rain forest.

But a second peep around the bathroom door proved I wasn't hallucinating. The snake was now coiled up, taking complete possession of my territory.

There had to be an easy way to take care of this unwelcome visitor, I reasoned. Grabbing a can of super-zap bug spray from the hall closet, I plotted the snake's demise. After I'd numbed it with the spray, I'd swoop it up and flush it away.

Clutching my little de-clawed Abbycat for security, I squared off in the doorway to squirt foam from afar. When the snake was well lathered, I retreated to the den, calmly turning on the morning news.

I congratulated myself on my bravery. The acclaim at work would go on and on: "How did you think of that?" "I'd have called the police." Or the paramedics. Or run screaming through the streets like a blithering idiot.

For good measure, I zapped/sprayed two more times, then grabbed essentials like toothbrush, curling iron, vitamin pills—and headed for the other bathroom. By this time the foggy house smelled like a bug-proofed picnic area. Forget breakfast.

Between consuming a week's quota of caffeine and getting ready for work, I crept to the half-bath door, time after time. The snake lay incredibly still as if it was finally done for. Now if I could just get it INTO something, then carry it out of the house like a glorious trophy. (Secretly, I had a dark desire to show it to someone, especially my husband, who had the nerve to be out of town for a three-day seminar.)

Brandishing a wastebasket and a toilet brush, I pitched headlong through the doorway just as the snake, not at all numbed from my efforts, began to slither across the floor, threatening to invade my bedroom.

That did it! I felt the adrenaline pumping. The only artillery left was the bathroom scale. With my hands shaking more from anger than fear, I lunged across the snake for the scale.

Bam! Bam! I pounded that scale down squarely with no mercy. Surely I'd drive that snake into whatever nether world there is for such detestable creatures.

I sensed victory at hand but also felt my courage cracking. Pouncing on the scale in triumph, I heard myself scream. "You've ruined my day, you son of a bitch!" Harder, harder I jumped. I didn't stop—even when the scale's needle wavered dizzily, then succumbed to zero.

Shuddering with scalp-prickling relief, I glanced in the mirror. Somehow the white suit I'd put on didn't seem appropriate for snake scraping. Soon enough to deal with what's *under* the scale when I get home from work. Besides, leaving it there is the only way I'll get anyone else in this household to believe this story.

A SAGA OF CUSTOMER SERVICE

What a nice touch. Someone in this big company really cares if I go away with my hands smelling as if I just overhauled a motor. While filling my gas tank, I'd spotted a handy dispenser of disposable plastic mittens nearby. Grabbing one, I stood ready to be protected when I removed the nozzle.

The pump clicked off. I looked at the dials and shuddered at the total. On my way from Cleveland to a conference in Dayton, I had foolishly chanced that gas prices might be lower in the central part of the state. Wrong!

Gripping the pump handle with my mittened hand, I lifted the nozzle. Wh-o-o-o-sh! Gasoline spouted geyser-like, covering me from the waist down.

Inside the station, the robot-like clerk told me that he'd "go out there in a few minutes." For what? To clean up the gasoline? After paying him, I complained again that the pump (No. 13) had malfunctioned somehow, that it sprayed gasoline all over my clothes, and the fumes would follow me to Dayton.

"Sometimes the lever sticks," he mumbled, looking at a spot on the back wall. "Somebody will come Monday and fix it." This was Thursday.

I headed for my car, making a wide swath around a man wearing a Go Bucks hat and brandishing a lighted cigar. In the time it took to record my gas purchase and mileage, the fumes from my clothing nearly gagged me. Thankfully, my wool slacks and sturdy leather shoes had protected my skin, but the rubber soles probably had absorbed the gasoline.

A familiar big-box department store, known for its clean restrooms, beckoned from across the road. Maybe I could wash away some of the odor from my clothes at least. I headed for the left rear of the store. There's some redemptive value for the homogenous boredom of chain stores. You always know where the restrooms are.

After fifteen fruitless minutes and a mountain of soggy paper towels, I was browsing the sportswear department. The best thing to do, I'd reasoned, was to pick up an inexpensive outfit, change clothes and be on my way. The only other clothes I had with me was a wool suit to wear to tomorrow's conference at the University of Dayton. While I scurried about trying to match a sweater with pants, I noticed other customers looking up at the ceiling with puzzled expressions, even alarm. When I reached the checkout, the topic of conversation centered on The Smell. Was there something wrong with the ventilating system? Should they evacuate the building?

"Both security and plant operations have been notified," the cashier was saying in a not-too-convincing tone.

Swallowing my pride, I confessed that I (or rather, my clothing) was the source of the offending fumes. Briefly, I explained my misfortune to put people at ease. One shopper sympathized but added, "You're lucky. I saw that happen to a guy, and the gasoline hit him in the face. They hauled him away in an ambulance." Another, a smartly dressed shopper who looked as if she should be shopping at Nordstrom's, gave me a down-the-nose stare as if to say she would never pump her own gas.

I scribbled my charge slip, scooped up my purchases and ducked out of the store. Nearby was another welcome sign—a McDonald's. At least, I wouldn't have to trek back through this store to do my quick change. And afterwards, I'd treat myself to my favorite panacea for jangled nerves and gnawing insecurity—a chocolate milkshake.

You can count on McDonald's, too, for adequate restrooms. (Maybe I should write a guidebook to restrooms in central Ohio.) The handicap stall afforded ample space for changing, and since I had the place to myself, I took advantage of soap and hot water to wash my feet and legs. I was managing okay with the automatic on-and-off faucet, but then I got to the drying part. Try drying your feet and legs at a hand dryer sometime.

The replacement clothes fit fine, so I rolled up the other slacks, sweater and socks into an odiferous bundle and asked for a large McDonald's bag along with my milkshake. The clerk didn't even faze me when he looked at my bundle and rolled his eyes. By this time, I was no longer up for explaining what had happened.

With my bundle stashed in the trunk, I again headed toward Dayton. But unfortunately, so were the fumes. My leather shoes must be the culprits. I'd tracked the gasoline onto the floor mats as well. With my eyes starting to smart and water, I chugged on the milkshake for solace, zapped open the sunroof and lowered the back windows.

After about ten miles, the sun disappeared. The milkshake was long gone, and my car's interior had all the coziness of Gasoline Alley. I punched on the heater, reached for a soothing CD of bird calls and babbling brooks and tried to find some humor in the situation. After all, I was headed to what was billed as the First Erma Bombeck Conference of American Humor.

Humor didn't come easily, so I consoled myself by mentally composing the letter I would write to the president of this company whose erupting gas pump had spoiled my day. Having once been given a year's free service by the telephone company, I'm a firm believer that we little guys do not have to be victimized by megamonsters of the corporate world. (The phone company had caused our household no end of bothersome calls one year by listing the number for the Mote family in the directory opposite Motel 6.)

Nowadays, the Internet helps us find these ubiquitous corporations that want to rule our lives. Their officers' names along with addresses, phone and fax numbers—even their corporate philosophies—are only a few mouse-clicks away. My letter borrowed a few choice phrases from this company's stated goals (such as "We aim to uphold the dignity and self-respect of our customers.") and accompanied it with bills for the clothing I'd purchased, the dry cleaning bills and replacement of the ruined shoes.

"You'll never hear anything," one gloom-and-doom friend declared. "You always pump gas at your own risk."

"Oh, ye of little faith," I told her. She hadn't read my carefully crafted, yet very honest letter.

Within two weeks, Ms. Risk Manager sent me a check for $152.25 and along with it a $100 gift certificate and profuse apology. She wrote that she hoped my future visits would be much more pleasant and that my confidence in their stores and their gas stations would be restored. She vowed to follow up with the station manager. Evidently, my letter was a convincing enough account of the incident. But then who would go to the trouble to invent such a scenario?

In my thank you note to Ms. Risk, I also made sure to mention what a nice gesture those plastic mittens are that protect customers' hands from gasoline spills.

PLEASE DON'T LANDSCAPE MY PLATE

I f you're close enough to read my bumper sticker, it says, "Banish Parsley." No, that's not a politician, nor is it a disease.

I'm talking about that ubiquitous, saucy sprig of greenery that wiggles at you from atop fillet of flounder, between pairs of eggs up, on mounds of delicate crepes or beside grease-encased ground rounds.

From Harbor Light, Maine, to Tombstone, Arizona, the green stuff is always with us. Especially in the semi-fast-food eateries—the

Shoneys, the Bob Evans, the waffle-pancake varieties, as well as the Mom-and-Pop-type diners.

Did you ever try to get rid of a piece of parsley? It's not polite to lay it on even a plastic-topped table. If you're lucky enough to have a saucer, you can try putting it there. But you can bet that your dining partner will soon be treated to the sight of squashed, coffee-soaked greenery clinging to the bottom of your cup. Nudge it discreetly to the side of your plate, Miss Manners would say. But the persistent stuff will somehow skid back into the eggs to become part of a gelatinous, orange/yellow mass.

My daughter, a health food enthusiast, expounds upon the nutritional value of parsley. She advises me to resolve my dilemma by eating it. Now it may be a magnificent source of iron ("needed by women your age, Mother"), but the thought of eating only one sprig of parsley makes my nose drip and my eyes smart. No other green has that pungent taste, that spongy feel. About like chewing a mouthful of highly seasoned rubber bands.

Great-aunt Sophie had a habit of "dressing up" any bowl of bland-looking vegetables—like mashed potatoes or creamed cauliflower—with a hearty shake of the paprika can. "Quick and colorful," she'd say. "Cheap, too." This must be the philosophy of restaurateurs who make sure their grill cooks keep a bowl of parsley at hand. That instant attempt at pseudo-elegance.

Parsley-hating has become an obsession with me. As I wait for my order, I wager with myself or my companions on the odds of a parsley-decked entrée. Glancing darkly at other diners' plates, all sporting bits of greenery, I wish I could banish that ignoble garnish forever with one evil glare.

Sometimes, though, I'm delighted by a trimming that shows a little love and concern for the patron. Like spiced crabapples that cost more or carrot curls that take more time. When these unique experiences occur—when I'm spared that audacious landscaping of my plate—I rejoice that there is still some creativity in the American food industry.

My server, who probably makes carrot curls during coffee breaks, gets twice the tip, and the comments on the back of my check reflect my sheer delight.

"Please Don't Landscape My Plate" originally appeared in *The Cleveland Plain Dealer* as "Hated parsley proves plague as a trimming."

FOR SERVICES RENDERED

Someday I'm going to plunk down an invoice for my services when I check out of a supermarket or discount store. It seems I spend considerable time not only serving myself but also assisting other customers—even employees.

I'm not referring to piling a wobbly-wheeled cart full of my own purchases and trundling it through a maze of jam-packed aisles. I'm polite when I interrupt the stockers' re-hash of last night's football game while I navigate around the tomato soup barricades. I don't even mind ambidextrously keeping a toddler granddaughter from stocking us up on candy bars, bubblegum and breath mints while I unload at the checkout.

Help-yourself shopping has been around for as long as I can remember. It's as much a part of consumerism as weekly specials and double coupons. Probably it got its start during World War II when high school grads began enlisting in the service and working in war plants instead of clerking in groceries and "dime stores."

Since then, consumers have been blessed with more and more features to make shopping attractive—floral shops, salad bars, video rentals, lottery tickets, kiddy play areas, branch banks—every week it seems there's something new. But the fact remains, we, the shoppers are doing considerably more of the actual work.

With the over-choice offered and the weekly price wars raging, shopping for a family these days requires a comparative shopping list resembling *Consumer's Digest*, plus a limitless supply of time and endurance. Since both of these commodities are in short supply when I shop on Saturday or on my way home from work, I stick to one supermarket or one discount store per shopping trip.

Because I'm a "regular customer" (recognizable only when I scan my debit card, not by my face), I'm incensed by the demands my self-service stores make upon me.

One day my two-year-old granddaughter Susie and I were trundling through a cavernous discount store. I stopped, mind-boggled, at a Family Glove Bar. Does one buy Toddler, Child, or One Size Fits All for a two-year old? Suddenly, a bright voice pierced my confusion. "How do you like this?" A sudden jab between my shoulders made me turn to face a tall, red-haired woman wearing a towering, green knitted hat and looking like a character from Dr. Seuss.

"Can you tell me what this looks like? It's hard to know…there's no mirror." Her earnestness quashed my first instinct to tell her what I thought the hat really looked like.

"It's a nice color with your hair," I said, proud of my tact. She went on rummaging through the pile of hats.

"How about this one?" I asked, pointing to a floppy beret that might make her look less as if she were scraping the ceiling. "Here, pull it forward a bit and to the side. There."

"Now for gloves." She plunged into the pile again. "Would these be okay with it?"

There were no kelly green gloves, so after a five-minute plunder, we finally switched to olive for both hat and gloves.

"Thanks for your help." She flashed a self-conscious smile. "I really hate shopping alone and not knowing how things look."

Smiling weakly, I looked at my watch. Fifteen minutes as a fashion consultant ought to be worth a few dollars. About as many as it would take to furnish a mirror.

In the supermarket meat section, while waiting for a response to "Push bell for service," I recently had another brief career. A bulky-framed man turned from the meat case, his face lined with discouragement. Catching my eye, he began pouring forth the woes of a single parent of four boys.

"No matter what I bring home for dinner, at least one of then wants a hamburger." His sad eyes didn't match his stern voice. "It's tough to be a father, mother, everything. If I do a good job at work, the house suffers. If I spend time with the boys, the job suffers. What's a man supposed to do?" Before two minutes passed, I knew the names of all four boys and that Johnny, the youngest, had chicken pox and hated his teacher.

Not ready to take on all these problems, I steered him to the pork chops. Over my shoulder, I saw the meat person finally appear. Frowning, she looked up and down the counter for the bell-ringer culprit, then shrugged and disappeared.

"You know," I touched the sleeve of the man's Cleveland Indians jacket, "we're our own worst critics. I bet you do a super job with your boys." He shook his head in abashed denial but looked pleased.

"How about trying some of these ready-stuffed pork chops for dinner?" I suggested. "My family loves them."

"You're a kind lady. I shouldn't have bothered you with my troubles." His broad, ethnic face shone with pleasure as he loaded his cart with enough pork chops for a Boy Scout troop.

Before he steered into Aisle 9—detergents, soaps, bleaches—he touched his hat brim. That rare, pleasant custom took the edge off my concern about missing the meat person.

Another fifteen minutes. This time as a menu planner? Family counselor? Maybe supermarket employees don't have credentials to handle domestic problems, but they could suggest stuffed pork chops, smile, and make a single parent feel less lonely.

Another job I qualify for at the supermarket is Trainer of Carryouts, or more aptly, Supervisor of Sackers. Carryout personnel only appear to assist customers who are visibly physically impaired. After years of fumbling to cope with overloaded and poorly loaded bags, I know precisely how to execute the sacking process. When I see frozen pies going in sideways or eggs shuffled to the bottom of a sack, it's time for me to step in with a bit of firm, kindly direction. Also, I double-check to see that the sack person sacks all my groceries. One time I arrived home without a twelve-dollar pork roast. Fortunately, a kind little Jewish lady found it sacked with her purchases and returned it promptly.

Once my purchases are sacked, paid for, check tendered or debit card scanned and approved, the sacker disappears into another check stand, diving bodily into another shopper's sacks. Sometimes someone orders me to have a good day, but more often it's more like a mumbled "There you go" as the checker, minus smile or eye contact, hands me the register tape.

I've accepted all this. Why would an able-bodied consumer like me, who's worked a full day and is now coping with a tired toddler and $112 dollars of groceries, need help to her car?

On one such occasion, though, my frazzled strand of patience zapped. After I'd fought my way through a lazy self-opening door, the front wheels of the cart hit a clod of slush. Suzy's farewell lollypop from the checkout counter flew into the dirty morass. Ditto for a bag that was teetering next to her on the seat.

Amid Suzy's wails, two dozen eggs began scrambling themselves on the grungy pavement. This time I'd had it! No matter how many double coupons my supermarket had just redeemed for me, I would NOT clean sidewalks. I grabbed Suzy and marched into the store to find the manager. Storming past the non-carryout, careless sack person, I ordered, "Watch that cart." I added, "Please." This kind of bold action is not my usual style.

At the customer service counter, I waited, shifting Suzy in her slippery nylon snowsuit from one hip to the other. She'd quit crying now, fascinated by the bleeps and falsetto voice coming from the nearby self-service scanner. The manager was explaining its use to a skeptical couple.

"You'll find it's going to be a real timesaver," he said, patting the conveyor with deference.

Finally, he approached me and I could state my case. Blinking behind owlish lenses, he turned to the intercom, his voice booming through the store. "Sacker, up front!" Before the wary U-scan customers had completed their purchases, my eggs were replaced and all sacks carefully repositioned in the cart. (It had magically been retrieved from the scrambled egg quagmire while I waited for the manager's attention.)

Mr. Bland-faced Manager solved my problem but was not the least bit apologetic. In fact, when I turned to thank him and add a few choice words about the importance of proper training of sack persons, he'd scurried away to attend to a malfunctioning lottery ticket dispenser.

Shoppers, it seems, must accept frustrations of self-service. They must inspect the eggs in the dairy case for cracks and count the popsicles to make sure the box contains a full dozen. They must also help train the employees and suffer through their learning experiences.

But I wonder how Mr. Bland would have reacted if I'd handed him a bill for my services. As a homemaker/grandparent/professional, I'd command a decent hourly rate.

PART TWO
LOOKING INWARD

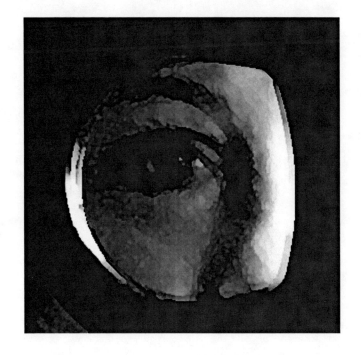

JEWELS IN MY CROWN

Kindly or unkindly, society once tagged unmarried ladies with the label, "Unclaimed Jewels." Perhaps this sounded kinder than "spinster." Looking back on my thirty-year career as an educator, I disagree with this label, for I claim a number of priceless jewels who shone brightly and guided my life from age ten to beyond seventy. Remembering these dedicated souls and their profound influence in my life, I call them more than jewels. These women were definitely heaven's gift to me, to guide me along life's journey. All were teachers. None ever married. They were wedded to their callings and their careers.

The day I retired from teaching, each of my six classes of high school seniors threw a party for me. One class presented me with a crown and dubbed me "Queen for a Day." When I took that crown off at the end of the day, I thought to myself that there should be jewels in it for each one of these dedicated teachers who had helped to lead me to this important day in my life.

Five brief profiles follow, describing the profound influence of each of these women upon various stages of my life: Miss Helenka Sagl, fourth grade teacher, University School, Bloomington, Indiana; Miss Helen Lotz, English teacher, Madison High School, Madison, Indiana; Dr. Dorothy Bucks, Professor of English, Hanover College; Miss Euzetta Foster, English teacher, Central Junior High School, Columbus, Indiana, and Sr. Bernadette Vetter, H.M., Vice President, The Center for Learning, Westlake, Ohio.

Miss Helenka Sagl
The University School
Bloomington, Indiana

Helenka Sagl led our fourth grade class onto the deserts of Africa and across the Alps of Switzerland. Social studies was her forte, and she integrated nearly every other subject into our particular country of focus. We produced murals of Alpine peaks and meadows, wrote plays about Dr. Doolittle in Egypt, sang African chants, and read biographies of world leaders from whatever country we studied. Miss Sagl wrote the book on interdisciplinary teaching before it became an educational buzzword.

We girls loved her stylish clothes (Why couldn't our mothers dress like Miss Sagl?). Her upswept hairdo looked like actress Ann Sheridan's, and her twinkling blue eyes and curling lashes were not lost on the boys in the class.

Helenka Sagl had a passion for creative expression and squeezed every bit of it that she could from us fourth graders. For a few of us who showed some ability in writing, for example, she would let us sit for unrestricted periods of time in a conference room to create a play that would later be performed for the entire school. In a story that I wrote about her (found in my mother's belongings) I wrote, "She (Miss Sagl) likes to use enormous words and likes for us to also. When we write stories she likes to see picture words."

Admittedly this was a very progressive school for the 1930s—a university lab school for training teachers. But it was here that a young beginning teacher planted seeds in the mind of a ten-year-old that would take root and eventually flower. Report cards at this school were not sterile letter grades but rather they were written evaluations of progress in each subject. After my mother's death a few years ago, I found some of these reports. In Miss Sagl's flowing penmanship, I read words of encouragement that must have stuck in my subconsciousness for decades. "Oral and Written Expression: Has vivid imagination and constructs written thoughts with unusual variety and coherence." (Sorry to say, these seeds lay dormant for many years during childrearing and schoolteaching.)

Interestingly enough, her comments for social studies were commendable as well, and social studies and English are the two subject areas in which I majored and eventually taught. But her comments weren't all glowing. "Artithmetic: Less skilled in this subject than in others. Perhaps due to fact that it does not interest her as much." (Even today I call that an understatement. I employ a bookkeeper but do my own ironing and cleaning.)

I often thought of Miss Sagl as I planned student activities that integrated social studies and English. She would have approved of the compassionate poems my vocational high school seniors wrote after sitting in the Cleveland Municipal Court for a day. Her interdisciplinary approach was reflected in students' vacation planning projects that combined use of maps, business letter writing, even math skills. Poems about their work, modeled on Langston Hughes' "Brass Spittoons," would have excited her. Along with on-the-job photos, these poems were featured in the school hallways and the local newspaper. "I feel like I'm famous," one poet-machinist remarked. A plus for academic studies amidst a vocational environment!

That young, vivacious teacher eventually served in the Women's Army Corps (WAC) and then returned to Indiana University and became Dr. Helen Sagl. An esteemed faculty member of the School of Education, she helped train other teachers to bring out the very best in their students—as she had intuitively done when she first taught at the IU lab school. She co-authored a book on teaching social studies through problem solving and established a scholarship for women elementary teachers.

Although I have no contact with anyone else who was in that fourth grade class, I'd wager there are others, particularly if they became teachers, who can recall Miss Sagl—her enthusiasm, her creative ideas, her gift for interweaving many facets of learning around a given subject. Her image glows in my collection of memories.

Miss Helen Lotz

Madison High School, Madison, Indiana

English teacher

"I don't care what you say, Miss Class President. You'll end up having Miss Lotz's prom –just like every other junior class." Bill R. was always so positive about everything. Sometimes he gave me a royal pain, but most of the time I was mesmerized by his intense blue-gray eyes and his beguiling dimples.

Three classes ahead of me in high school, he'd already graduated, done a stint in the Air Force and was headed to Indiana University next fall. He was biding his time working, as he had during high school, as a desk clerk at the inn my father managed.

"This year we'll do things differently," I declared trying to match Bill's confident tone. But he shook his head, turned his back, and kept on rolling quarters. He'd been president of his class, too, and he knew what it was to do battle with Miss Lotz.

Miss Helen Lotz, the perennial junior class sponsor, had taught English to a couple of generations by the time I reached her sunny corner classroom. When I was elected junior class president at the beginning of the year, I'd brashly declared our class would do something radically different for our prom. No more crepe paper streamers stapled from wires strung around the gym floor. Oh, no. My friends and I were dreaming up a themed prom. Something like "Moonlight and Roses" with a ceiling of thousands of crepe paper roses and a silver-spangled moon rising behind the throne of the prom king and queen.

As today's last class had ended, Miss Lotz beckoned to me with one of her ringless fingers. "Patsy, I just want to give you an idea of the arrangements for the prom before our next class meeting." She smiled, flashing her bridgework. Miss Lotz must spend a lot of time in the dentist's chair, I thought. Too bad he can't whiten up those front teeth. They almost match her tired, dyed blonde hair.

"All right," I said meekly, stifling my cruel thoughts. I stood next to her chair like an obedient servant. The early spring air floated in through the open windows, canceling out the pungent odor of chalk dust and oiled wood floors. All I wanted to do was rush through this ordeal and get up to Rogers' Drug Store to be with my friends.

As she turned the pages of a Double Q notebook, I swear I heard them crackle with age. "Now, Mr. Forry will hang the wires from each corner…"she pointed to a faded diagram.

A vicious urge gripped me. It was all I could do to keep from slamming my five-pound *Literature and Life in America* book down on top of her ancient notebook….

Well, I didn't do it, and "Moonlight and Roses" didn't happen either. I did learn to hold my tongue but disagree politely on a few points. And I was able to brag to Bill R. that we got the silvery moon even though onlookers at the prom still had to peer at us through those everlasting crepe paper streamers. Seems we never found enough volunteers to make the thousands of crepe paper roses.

During my senior year, Miss Lotz and I would sometimes exchange serious words about English class—usually after she'd handed back a theme marked "Nicely expressed" or "Do not recopy" in her prim, teacher-like script. She was never lavish with her praise even if it was an A paper.

"You should be a teacher, Patsy," she declared one day, again keeping me from the gang and Rogers' Corner. She looked at me earnestly, her eyes like pools of watered-down blue ink behind their thick lenses. I ducked my head and studied the tips of my saddle shoes. All I could think was *I don't want to turn out like you, lady.*

She was straightening her desk as she talked—a pile of papers stacked on the left, books between bookends in a military row. "Your love of reading is evident, you write well and you are a leader in your class."

She knows my love of reading, all right. I sit right there in the front row and read my own books when she's reading aloud to the class the last ten minutes of the day. I did it all through my junior year, too. I *hated* being read to, but the rest of the class seemed to like it. They were all lapping up *Ivanhoe*, while I persisted in reading *Vanity Fair*. Funny thing, Miss Lotz never once told me to put my own book away, even though I realize now I was being incredibly rude.

Well, despite my rebellious attitude, I did become a teacher—of English. I never went back to see Miss Lotz to tell her so, but I'm sure she knew. Ours was a small town. But I wish I'd told her how learning to outline like she taught us was an invaluable skill that saw me through years of note taking in college and graduate school. It helped me think in an orderly fashion and be a better listener. And even if I was bored during a lecture, I could always get caught up in creating a great outline while feigning great interest.

Once I became a teacher, I often pictured Miss Lotz, tacking up pictures of Emily Dickinson's home or of Walt Whitman or Edgar Allan Poe on a small bulletin board just inside the classroom door. She would point to these pictures and talk about the authors as if they were her friends. She challenged us to want to know them better. As a beginning teacher, my first request to my principal was for a BIG bulletin board. Big, all right. I walked in one morning to find a 4 x 8-foot monster on the back wall that became a chore to keep filled with current and meaningful material.

Miss Lotz always sat at her desk when she taught—like a grand duchess. Her navy blue dress (the only color I associate with her) usually had a prim, neat collar and a few flakes of dandruff on the shoulders. But there was no question of class control. She had it, instinctively. And at a moment's notice she could quote lines from Keats or Coleridge or from Poe or Whitman. Just seeing any of those names brings up the memory of Miss Lotz's expressive voice. I never mastered that ability that she had—to quote from memory, pulling lines out of thin air, it seemed. Too many other roles must have crowded their demands into my consciousness—wife, mother, department chairman, Cub Scout Den mother, Sunday School teacher....

But I'm sorry I never went to see Miss Lotz. I knew where she lived with her aged mother in that little apartment over her brother's shoe repair shop. I wish I'd let her know how much I learned from her and what an inspiration she was to me—in spite of myself.

Dr. Dorothy S. Bucks
Professor of English
Hanover College
Hanover, Indiana

She was a professor at Hanover College for more than a quarter century, but I sat in her classroom overlooking the Ohio River's famous S-curve for only one semester. Yet, that one course yielded far more than three hours credit; it kindled my interest in what would become a lifelong devotion to experiencing live theater.

Dr. Dorothy Bucks, a passionate theater lover, sat calmly, facing a circle of twelve students enrolled in Modern Drama. It was not a class in acting; instead, we read an assigned play before each class meeting and discussed it as literature that, in the poet's words, "holds a mirror up to mankind."

Always impeccably dressed in a tailored suit with tasteful jewelry, Dr. Bucks sat, poised, ankles crossed, wearing Cuban-heeled suede oxfords, as she led us through in-depth discussions of great gems of the theater. With no visuals other than an occasional playbill she passed around the class, Dr. Bucks brought these characters to life on the imaginary stage of our classroom.

A tall, stately woman, I think of her yet as being the epitome of unassuming confidence and dignified composure. Most, if not all of the plays, she had seen performed. Eloquently, she helped us experience the pain and loneliness of a physically challenged Laura in *The Glass Menagerie*, the false bravado and inevitable failure of Willy Loman in *Death of a Salesman,* the chilling effects of prejudice on the judicial system in *Twelve Angry Men.*

Those plays, incidentally, were fairly recent at that time but were destined to become perennial offerings on American stages. Earlier plays, such as O'Neill's *Beyond the Horizon,* had us exploring the frustration of a triangular love affair not unlike what would openly threaten many modern families as the divorce rate began to climb. In Ibsen's *A Doll's House*, we encountered an early commentary on women's rights and self-expression. These dramatists were harbingers of social changes that our generation would face as graduates of the 1950s. Though most of us would spend nearly a decade settling into our pseudo-idyllic suburban surroundings, the awareness of these dilemmas brought to life in Dr. Bucks' Modern Drama classroom smoldered in our consciousness; eventually we would become personally involved in some of these same struggles.

In her calm manner and well-modulated voice, Miss Bucks (as she was then known although she had an earned doctorate) brought out the best in each of us, gently nudging us to think critically and subtly helping us to shed our own prejudices. Each of the plays in the syllabus would demonstrate what had been the subject of Dorothy Bucks' dissertation at Northwestern University some years earlier—that the stage could become a vehicle by which to explore social problems, even in an academic environment. This was an idea then in its infancy.

This premise fit perfectly into my double major of English and the social sciences. As a teacher three decades later, I developed a course in American Theater for seniors at a vocational high school. Graduation required specific credits in English, but most of these students were more interested in their vocational classes, preparing them for a trade in auto mechanics, for example, or cosmetology or medical assisting. This American Theater class became a class in play-reading and discussion. Students read assigned roles from passages from well-known American plays—some of the same ones I had read with Miss Bucks.

Many students in that American Theater course, though perhaps reluctant readers, became caught up in the lives of the characters and discussed their problems in the light of American life, applying the characters' dilemmas to their own lives. Force-fed on television since their playpen days, these often blasé and indifferent young people sat, virtually starry-eyed and open-mouthed, when we attended student matinees at the Cleveland Play House. Sitting close enough almost to participate in live drama has a mesmerizing effect.

I wish I could send Dr. Bucks a copy of my most recent book, *Cleveland's Playhouse Square* (Arcadia Publishing 2006). Detailing and illustrating the largest theater restoration in the world, this book is testimony to my personal enthusiasm for live theater, first instilled by that long-ago class in Modern Drama.

And how I would like to be among Hanover students who came after me who benefited from Dr. Bucks' innovative Shakespeare-in-England course. Taught every other spring since the mid-1960s, each time it was offered, despite the additional cost, some students had to be told "no." Wrote one student for *The Hanoverian* alumni bulletin, "The entire trip was a fantastic experience made possible by the amazing planning of Dr. Bucks...Each student was introduced to

England in the fullest sense—historically, culturally, and socially so that the impact was most complete."

After she retired in 1973, Dr. Bucks remained in her home near the Hanover campus. She continued to participate in and wield a quiet influence upon the close-knit life of the college community. Her Shakespeare-in-England course and many of the college-wide curricular changes she initiated continued.

Upon her ninetieth birthday, the college and the community honored her, and alumni also could send greetings. Along with my good wishes, I sent her a copy of my biography of television pioneer news analyst, Dorothy Fuldheim. Dr. Bucks' acknowledgment was far more than a brief thank you. Writing in longhand, she told of her interest in following my writing activities through the years. She wrote that she had purchased as gifts five copies of my first book, *Showers of Blessings*, co-authored with Alma D. Hall. Mrs. Hall had been a well-loved employee of the college and had worked many years earlier at Clifty Inn where my father was the innkeeper.

When Dr. Dorothy Bucks died in 2002, her estate created an endowment fund for international studies. Her generosity is making a tangible difference for Hanover students and will impact generations to come.

I know how much my life has been incredibly enriched from sitting—no, participating—in Dr. Dorothy Bucks' classroom three times a week for only one semester. I feel blessed. Not only did she bequeath to me her infectious love of the theater, but also, in my own thirty years as an educator, I found myself emulating her interdisciplinary approach to teaching and her emphasis on helping students to develop critical thinking skills.

Her obituary stated that there were "no immediate survivors." Yet, as teachers are often told that their influence extends far beyond their comprehension, so Dorothy Bucks left a legacy to generations of

Hanover alumni; she was an exemplary educator in her methods and one who inspired each student she taught with a love of literature and the theater.

We are all her beneficiaries.

Patricia Mote

Miss Euzetta Foster

Central Junior High School

Columbus, Indiana

She taught reading to reluctant teenagers. No, she inspired her students to WANT to read. And Euzetta Foster took me by the hand and made me realize there was more to teaching than following a syllabus or issuing letter grades.

Every lanky, pimply-faced ninth grader who walked into her reading lab was a challenge to Miss Foster. To see her students increase their reading speed and comprehension were the stated goals of her program. But Miss Foster could be counted on to dispense wisdom and compassion as well as reading techniques. She could persuade an overweight girl to go to the school nurse for counseling, or she'd find a winter coat for another who was shivering in a lightweight sweater in December. When a basketball player admitted to her that his stepfather was responsible for his bruised face, Miss Foster and the basketball coach teamed up to report the incident to juvenile authorities.

I had returned to full-time teaching after being at home with my three children for ten years. There was a lot to learn besides how to balance career and family demands. This community was regarded as a "lighthouse" district in the state, a leader in innovative delivery of education. After only a couple of years of part-time teaching and one year full-time in one of the junior high schools, I found myself wearing the title of department chair. Seven teachers, all with many years of experience, made up my department. Realistically, I felt I'd been offered the job because the administrative higher-ups saw me as a potential innovator; I was newly returned to teaching and not set in my ways as a teacher.

Truly, I had my work cut out for me. Attempting to get some of the dear ladies in my department to change their methods was an uphill battle. The idea of integrating vocabulary and grammar lessons with the study of literature was daunting for them. More than once, a department meeting involved testy complaints from some of them and unyielding demands from me. Afterwards, Euzetta Foster would take me aside. "Be gentler," she would advise. "Kathryn (one of the most vocally resistant of the department) has a right to her feelings. You can't expect everyone to change overnight." She'd pat my shaking hand with her freckled one, her soft brown eyes reflecting empathy for my situation as well as for our colleagues.

Though only a few years away from retirement, Euzetta sprinted down the hallways in her housedress and corrective shoes with nearly the same speed as she'd dribbled a basketball as a student at this very same school fifty years earlier. But nothing escaped her. A too-amorous couple by the lockers or an overly aggressive student threatening another would get quiet but firm reprimands. Her colleagues as well were not immune from her disapproval. Of one teacher she'd mentored who had been promoted to administrator, she remarked, "I hope he doesn't forget whose shoulders he stood on."

After Euzetta had retired, I was forced to a leave of absence due to illness. It was then I saw another side of this remarkable lady. During my convalescence, I rode my bike around town and could stop without invitation at Euzetta's home. She and her sister Bessie, a retired telephone operator, lived with their aged but amiable dog in the house where they were born. Mid-mornings, I'd often find them at their oilcloth-covered kitchen table, still in their pajamas. Beneath a cloud of smoke from unfiltered Camels, they'd dress dolls to give away to charity. As I drank strong black coffee and watched them work, Euzetta doled out homespun wisdom and shared her no-nonsense approach to life. She helped me hurdle barriers to wellness I was trying to scale and did more to restore the confidence that my illness had damaged than all the bottles of pills my doctors prescribed.

Years later, after I'd moved to another state, I happened to be visiting my former hometown. I had hoped perhaps to visit Euzetta. But that very day, the local paper carried her obituary. She had died peacefully, outliving her sister Bessie. When I called at the funeral home, I met my former principal there. We hugged each other as we stood before our dear friend, agreeing that teachers like Euzetta were God's gift to humankind. Humbly, we gave thanks for our good fortune to have been her colleagues and influenced by her example.

Sister Bernadette Vetter, H.M.

The Center for Learning

Westlake, Ohio

I was weary of being a mentor to the beginning English teachers my vocational high school kept hiring. Retirement was beckoning invitingly, only a few years away. I longed for a sympathetic heart to thrust my frustrations upon, someone to challenge my waning enthusiasm for my profession. In a fortuitous opportunity, I came under the influence of Sister Bernadette Vetter, co-founder and vice president of the Center for Learning with editorial offices then in nearby Rocky River, Ohio.

As a freelance writer for the Center, I spent frequent after-school planning sessions in Sr. Bernadette's calming presence. The walls of books and inspirational art seemed to embrace us and lifted my spirits. She would chuckle warmly when telling an amusing story as we'd begin our meetings. Thriving on politics, her eyes snapped as she spoke in her uniquely dramatic manner of her scorn for the then-current administration in Washington. An ardent Democrat, her voice had trembled with excitement when she called to ask me to write a curriculum guide for John F. Kennedy's *Profiles in Courage*.

Sister B's bobbed hair and fringed bangs gave her a little-girl look that complemented her wonder and delight in life. Her eyes would dance merrily at a political joke or soften with empathy listening to my frequent frustrations with teaching reluctant teenagers. A gentle spirit, Sr. Bernadette brought calm and direction to my professional life at a critical time. For the first time in decades, I had found a professional mentor as well as a dear and trusted friend.

About the time I was graduating from college, Sister Bernadette had become founding principal of Magnificat High School for girls in suburban Cleveland. There she and her colleague, Sister Rose Schaffer, founded the Center for Learning in 1970 in a tiny room. "About the size of a broom closet," she once said. The Center is a non-profit educational publishing house devoted to curriculum writing for teachers by teachers in the areas of English, social studies and religion.

By the time one of its brochures came across my desk in the 1980s, the Center was well established and nationally respected. Its mission was to be a producer of values-based materials. Novels, for example, would not only pursue a story line, but students would also apply the characters' experiences to their own lives and times. Writers of all faiths were welcomed to write the English and social studies materials.

The eight books of teaching materials I eventually wrote for the Center drew upon all of the creativity I could muster. They were more challenging intellectually than any graduate course in education I ever had, and Sister Bernadette's guiding spirit is reflected in each of them. The thrill of knowing my materials would be used by teachers all over the country, in fact, internationally, motivated me as well. I still delight in seeing my books described in the Center's catalogs.

Although Sister Bernadette and my husband Newton never met, they had a Mutual Admiration Society by telephone. When she would call my home, often ten minutes or more went by as the two of them chatted about politics, sports or an upcoming trip Newt and I had planned. Then he would call me to speak with "the good Sister" as he always referred to her. I sent her a small picture of Newt and me taken on our twenty-fifth anniversary. She wrote, "Your picture is truly revealing of the great match you two are!!" She always rejoiced in the uniqueness of our blended family and shared Newt's and my belief that our mid-life second marriage was a God-given gift.

I feel I had a chance to make a gift to Sr. Bernadette indirectly. When I was researching the life of Cleveland's legendary television news personality Dorothy Fuldheim, I learned from Sr. Bernadette that she had once been interviewed by Dorothy Fuldheim. She shared with me a copy of the videotape of that remarkable interview. By including portions of it in my Fuldheim biography, published in 1997, I was able to introduce thousands of readers to Sister Bernadette's testimony of faith and her joyous spirit.

> "I expected it (the interview) to focus on education," Sister Bernadette recalled. But in her no-nonsense manner, Dorothy disposed of education as a topic by observing that there is so much more for people to learn nowadays. Then she focused her laser-like questions on matters of the spirit. "Will we find out the whole mystery of the universe?"

> Sister Bernadette's answer was swift and confident. "Certain key people help us to discover ourselves on our spiritual journey. Life is a mystery to be lived. We have to keep tuned into other people's hearts to find Him. Our relationship with God keeps growing" .....

The nun, who was not wearing a habit but was dressed in a simple business suit, quietly emphasized her belief in the human need for reflection, for self-discovery; Dorothy Fuldheim, on the other hand, focused upon the vast amount of new knowledge there is today and the need to know and to unlock the secret of the universe.

Suddenly, the hostess demanded of her guest, "Are you as happy as you seem? How long have you been a nun?"

"Why, Dorothy," Sister Bernadette's face brightened. "I've been a nun for forty-five years."

Dorothy pressed on. "And would you live your life the same way again?"

"Yes, Dorothy." There was not a moment's hesitation. "Exactly the same."

"And are you happy because you established your relationship with God a long time ago?" Dorothy questioned.

"Yes," Sister Bernadette answered, hastening to add, "but it keeps growing."

"Interesting. Interesting." Dorothy scrutinized the nun's radiant face as if she hoped to find the key to a vast secret. "You are a happy person, one of the happiest I've ever talked to."

Reprinted from *Dorothy Fuldheim: The FIRST First Lady of Television News*© Patricia Mote 1997.

When her health failed, Sister Bernadette went to live with her Sisters of Humility of Mary at the mother house in Villa Maria, Pennsylvania. Though I still receive Christmas greetings and prayers from the Center for Learning, they are no longer in Sister B's graceful, flowing hand. The intellectual challenges she offered me enriched my adult life, and her zest for living lifted my spirit. I treasure the words from her last note to me: "Do know that you are never forgotten, and we will always in touch."

As this book was in production, Sister Bernadette Vetter went to join the saints and Christ and the Blessed Mother to whom her life was dedicated. Her joyous and endearing spirit will remain with me always.

How privileged I was that each of these five talented, dedicated women helped shape my life and shepherded my journey. Each one blessed me with her unique talents, her wisdom, and her example of a wise and caring professional.

INFLUENCE FROM ACROSS THE AISLE AND OVER THE DECADES

Her name was Marie. She died in her own home, at 94, outliving her husband—a beloved judge—and one of their three children. Reading her obituary in my university's newsletter set off a flood of memories from my early childhood.

A vivid image of Marie surfaces. Her wispy-veiled, Depression-era hat dipped over one of her dark, flashing eyes. In her tailored dress with crocheted collar, she sat, poised as a princess, at a sturdy oak library table. Radiators sizzled and pale winter sunlight forced its way through leaded church parlor windows. Marie led a group of thirty-some women, seated in creaking folding chairs, in their creed: "I am only one, but I am one. I cannot do everything, but I can do something; and what I can do, that I ought to do; and what I ought to do, by the grace of God, I shall do." Their dedicated voices, buried in my consciousness for decades, speak even now with stereo-like resonance.

My mother attended the Women's Association faithfully the second Saturday of every month, and, as I was then an only child whose father worked on Saturdays, so did I. Babysitter was an unknown word, even if there'd been money for one. Sitting on the floor at my mother's feet, I would absently comb my Shirley Temple doll's hair.

At the same time I would study Marie. Her voice seemed to smile, somehow, even though the words were serious. She spoke calmly, with just enough emphasis to make me know she meant what she said, yet she was never stagey or affected. Little did I imagine, until I read of

Marie's death, how clearly I could recall those Women's Association meetings and the church life of my youth. Only now do I realize how indelibly those experiences affected my life.

The church itself was awesome in the true sense of the word. Built of native Indiana limestone, its vaulted ceiling and its Gothic arches thrilled me. The hanging lamps along the side aisles looked like upside-down crowns. No wonder we sang songs like "Crown Him with Many Crowns" and "Come Thou Almighty King." The part of church I liked and understood best was when the choir came down the aisle. There were two other ladies I liked to watch: Miss Sarah and Miss Esther, always first and in perfect step, Miss Sarah's powerful soprano blending with Miss Esther's sturdy, perfect-pitch alto. Every Sunday, we sang the same song when they marched in—"Holy, Holy, Holy." I loved the line about ". . . casting down their golden crowns around the glassy sea," I tried to draw that, but my crowns looked like jagged teeth sitting on a tabletop.

During the week, my playmates and I would play "church" in the back yard. Always, I'd want to be Miss Sarah, and I'd try to imitate her angelic expression and her proud posture as we "processed" toward our grape-arbor sanctuary. I was happy when Miss Sarah married one of the men in the choir whose wife had died, but I never thought it was right they couldn't march down the aisle together on Sundays.

I went on admiring Miss Sarah and tried to learn to call her Mrs. Franklin in my mind. Like Marie, she scarcely knew who I was. She probably had no idea that a wide-eyed, restless youngster seated between her parents every Sunday watched her every move. How mysterious are the processes of the human mind! These women truly inspired me—a very young girl—as I observed them, admired them, imitated them.

Only when I read Marie's obituary, more than a half-century later, and recalled her grace and charm so vividly, did I recognize how she, as well as Miss Sarah, had been God-given role-models for me at a very impressionable age. Why couldn't these memories have crowded their way into my consciousness years ago—when I was the one who was singing in church choirs, working with young people in youth groups, teaching Sunday school and vacation church school? Then young children were not scurried out of the sanctuary before the sermon. They still fidgeted in the pews, spilled grape juice, and probably imagined the contemporary sanctuary to be a spaceship. People they saw at church each Sunday became life models, even though during the week they competed with Mary Tyler Moore and Donna Reed.

Did I project to children any qualities worthy of copying as Marie and Miss Sarah had done for me? I thought of Sunday mornings when I'd caught myself nodding, in full view in the choir loft after staying out late the night before or getting up and down all night with a sick child. What about the times I'd taught Sunday school when I wasn't as prepared as I should have been? Or do I, even now, use the organ prelude as a time for chit-chat instead of preparation for worship? And do I get caught up in after-church gossip within hearing of others, including young people?

When we're working directly with children—teaching, advising—we're sharply aware of our influence. Before we hit our middle years, they admire our clothing, and they have crushes on us. As the years creep up on us, we become their mother/father confessors. "I wish my mother understood me like you do," younger people complain, loading us with their dilemmas, hanging on to our pearls of wisdom. But whether we're directly involved with young people or have only an indirect or casual contact with them, our words and actions are on display. In recognizing our chance to influence young people positively, we would do well to emulate the model described in the Epilogue to Proverbs 31:25-27, 30 quoted here generically as The Wife and Husband of Noble Character:

They are clothed with strength and dignity;
they can laugh at the days to come.
They speak with wisdom,
and faithful instruction is on their tongues.
Charm is deceptive and beauty is fleeting;
but a woman or man who fears the Lord is to be praised.

Somehow, I think Marie and Sarah were both persons of noble character, and so were their husbands. Times were hard then, but life was simpler. In today's frenzied living, many women strive to be not only wives and mothers of noble character but also competent lawyers and construction workers, teachers and engineers. Fathers are no longer the sole providers for and absolute rulers of a household; many share a more intimate role in the caregiving and nurturing of their children than fathers of earlier generations; thousands of single parents share or have total custody of their children.

Thus, our example is magnified. Our influence as role models for children and youth must reach much farther than across the aisle on Sunday morning. If we are truly our brother's (and our sister's) keeper, then we also must shoulder a responsibility for the children of those brothers and sisters whenever and wherever the chance exists. The competition—that of unwholesome models—threatens to permeate and engulf our entire society.

Indeed, we cannot do everything, but we can do something: show our own children and the youth of our churches and communities the most fervent, committed examples of Christian adults that we can be.

CARPE DIEM

Some years ago, actor Robin Williams made a name for himself by seizing days. In the movie *Dead Poets Society*, Williams, as an idealistic, idolized professor, daily urged his preppy charges to suck the marrow of their lives and do things worthy of their time. He quoted the classics, particularly the poet Horace's Ode: "Seize the day," he would burble theatrically. "Put no trust in the morrow."

Horace had plenty of time to seize days. He was a noble Roman who owned slaves to fan him with olive branches and to stomp grapes for his wine. And life was not all that fast-paced at the boys' prep school in *Dead Poets Society* either.

But here we are, now well into another millennium. We don't have time to seize whole days to enlighten our existence or help uphold the pillars of society. Our days are crammed with commitments and cluttered with choices.

Maybe we should update Horace's ode to read "Carpe momenta" (Seize the moments). Today, we have to grab at whatever snippets of time we can if we want to "stretch" our beings, to grow in awareness and thereby do something more than give lip service to those overworked words—"kinder," "gentler" and "family values." Sometimes, brief but indelible moments can propel us beyond the too-often humdrum pattern of our daily lives and make us feel we're truly contributing threads to society's fabric.

We've all learned ways to steal time. Multi-task, it's called today. We juggle several balls at once to cope with the demands of fast-paced living. Everyone knows you can balance your checkbook or clean out your desk drawers while on hold with customer service or while trying to make a doctor's appointment. Or that you can cook a whole meal during TV commercials. But can we look beyond the "must-do" level? How do we snatch bits of time to get in tune with the rhythm of the universe?

First, we could get rid of the perennial "around to it" mindset and replace it with a "now do it!" attitude. We can seize upon an idea or an action when it strikes us. Instead of musing, *I haven't seen my elderly neighbors since this snowstorm began. I wonder how they are*, why not seize a few moments and make a phone call?

Rather than berating yourself, *I ought to do something with that tacky-looking corner of the yard*, try grabbing a pencil and paper and sketching a perennial bed—or make a phone call to a landscape contractor. If you're having a trying day, take time to watch children playing. Their vitality will give you a lift. Promise yourself that every day you'll write a note to a shut-in, a student away at school or a person in military service. Give a few words of praise to people who do routine tasks for you—the school crossing guard, delivery people, the salad bar cleaner.

Just letting that person with only a frozen pizza and a half-gallon of ice cream go ahead of you at the supermarket checkout will get you started seizing moments. From there on, you'll surprise yourself at how many opportunities leap at you in a day's time.

Carpe Diem previously appeared in *The Cleveland Plain Dealer* titled Never mind day; seize moment.

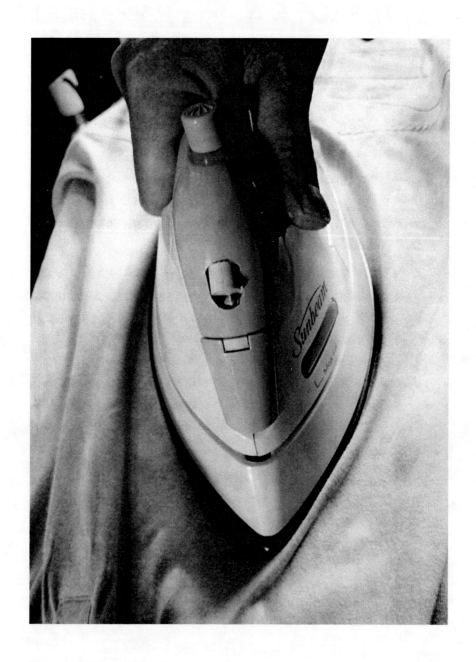

SMOOTHING OUT THE WRINKLES

Mother always said, "Just like the poor, ironing will always be with us." Back in my June Cleaver-early-married days I proudly disputed her prediction by performing my Tuesday ritual at the ironing board with naïve pleasure. While Ma Perkins and Helen Trent sidestepped disasters and solved their dilemmas on my tinny kitchen radio, I smoothed wrinkles from carefully dampened and starched white shirts and pinafores. Neither the women's movement nor the economic crunch made me feel guilty that I had abandoned a career for marriage and a GI-loan, pre-fab home in suburbia.

This was definite "me-time." The wearers of the shirts and pinafores were at work or napping, respectively. Without benefit of steam iron, spray starch or wash-and-wear, I actually looked forward to Tuesday afternoons. Admittedly, it was a cozier chore in dead of winter than on humid August days, but it was a once-a-week, not-to-be-put-off task. I could daydream or write poems in my head. Or if I had a problem of my own, I'd sift through the pros and cons, weigh my options, search for answers. The steady smoothing-out of the fabrics beneath my iron, the lengthening row of garments on hangers in the doorway, and the eventual sight of the bottom of the ironing basket were reassuring; there would be an orderly solution to whatever my current dilemma happened to be.

When my mother reached 85, she changed her tune; she declared that if it didn't seem like something of a sacrilege, thanks to easy-care fabrics and her casual life-style, she could get along for the rest of her days without her iron and ironing board. And luckily for her, ironing is only for people with strong backs, not often possessed by octogenarians.

I disciplined myself recently to keep a long-overdue appointment with an ironing basket. It was overflowing with shirts and slacks I'd forgotten we owned. As I set up my ironing board, I didn't bother to turn on the television; I had a problem more discouraging than any I cared to witness on the daytime soaps. I'd been treated unfairly, I thought, by my boss, a person whom I deeply respected. Should I retaliate, quit, forgive?

I was alone in the house. There were no white shirts or pinafores in my basket, the wearers of those having retired or become mothers, respectively. While the air conditioner hummed, punctuated by the steam iron's frequent hiss, my frantic brain raced from one episode to another in the previous day's scenario, just as it had for most of the night before.

Plodding steadily through the pile of ironing, I marveled that I was actually accomplishing something in spite of still-seething anger. The steam iron's path was creating some order in my day, at least. In a state of mind that seemed to span several decades, I smoothed and straightened, pleated and pressed. As the row of shirts and slacks hanging in the doorway grew longer, my vengeful thoughts began to subside without my realizing it.

Strangely, I felt I was standing in the kitchen of that tiny ranch home of so many years ago. Those had been lean years with problems that sometimes out-soaped the soaps. Just as I'd wrestled through my young-married-with-children problems at the ironing board then, so here I was, in all the supposed wisdom of my mature years, doing the same thing. So real did it seem, I half-expected to hear a child calling from the bedroom as she woke from her nap.

But instead of a child's voice, it was my father's I could hear now. One of his favorite pearls of wisdom jarred me back to the present. "This, too, shall pass." Sometimes that used to irritate me when he'd say it. So simplistic, so glib, it sounded. But he believed it, he lived it, and, in my heart, I knew it was so. Slamming the steam iron down on the waistband of a pair of slacks, I ignored the scalding water that splashed out on my hand, and the tears I felt welling up. Tough as it was, I knew forgiveness was my only choice.

When I hung the freshly ironed clothes in our closets, I felt wrapped in a cocoon of relief. Not because I'd finished the ironing at last, but that I'd deliberately worked through my pain and frustration.

That forced attachment to a steady, useful but mindless activity must make standing at the ironing board a unique place for getting one's head on straight. Maybe if those of us who juggle several roles and try to meet the demands of many people would make more frequent appointments with the ironing board, we'd have less need for tranquillizers and appointments with therapists.

Smoothing Out the Wrinkles previously appeared in *Plus 50 Magazine*.

STREETS OF HEAVEN

Approaching Indiana on Interstate 70, the cold driving rain that had pelted down in Columbus, Ohio, had given way to an occasional drizzle. Infrequent bursts of sunlight flashed across the mottled sky. The flat, ribbon-like I-70 seemed to head directly for purplish-blue banks of clouds stretching low just above the horizon.

It was nearly the end of the year—2001, a year of both national and personal tragedy. Just as I was putting my personal life into something of a skewed order after my husband's sudden death in March, then came 9-11, pouring sorrow and fear into the very core of our nation's being.

At a rest stop I turned down the CD of march music I'd been playing to keep alert. Feeling stuffed from the Sunday buffet meal I'd enjoyed with my son and his family in Columbus, I was tempted to nap, but a brief stop to make a phone call would have to do if I was to reach Indy before dark.

Back on the road with the marches thrumping once again, I could see now-and-again shafts of sunlight streaming down from behind darkening, rumpled clouds. The same low banks of clouds lay across the horizon, lighter now as sunset neared. When "The Washington Post March" signaled the end of the CD, I realized that my favorite number, "Le Regiment" (the Script Ohio march) must have played while I was making my phone call. I punched up number 10 so I could hear it.

As if on cue with the opening bars, the dark clouds above the stubbled cornfields shifted, and glorious golden shafts poured down upon the striated layers of clouds now spanning the horizon. "Streets of heaven," I heard myself say aloud. As always, "Le Regiment" lifts my spirits, but this time it seemed to raise me up to march along those streets. They were brilliant now, row upon row. There were no people, for this was not a vision. But I could imagine the people…and in my head, I could hear my dear husband's voice "playing" his "E-fer" (E-flat cornet) part as he always did.

I continued driving, but the splendor before me was dazzling, filling my eyes with tears of awe and joy. "Thank you, God," I whispered, "for this blessed assurance of your nearness. You have brought my dear husband, my soul mate who lives now with you, very close to me, here on this highway that we've traveled together so many times."

This was as precious a Christmas gift as I could receive.

December 23, 2001

PART THREE
A BACKWARD LOOK

THE VOICE OF THE THIRTIES

My mother would undoubtedly say that the purchase of her electric refrigerator was the most blessed and miraculous event in our household since that of my birth a few years before. Practically speaking, this was true; its comforting hum in our kitchen marked the end of moldy cheese and sour milk and the beginning of an era of frozen desserts and unlimited ice cubes.

For me to single out the most exciting event of my grade-school years is not difficult. The dismal days of the Depression were just receding, and children savored even little pleasures. For instance, the first time my mother let me go to the grocery store alone, I walked the two blocks carrying that quart milk bottle as if the dime jingling inside were an offering to the gods.

If such a small pleasure can be recalled so vividly, you can imagine, then, how momentous an occasion the arrival of our first radio was! Far more excited about this event than I had been about the refrigerator, I fidgeted on the porch swing as my father uncrated this long-saved-for wonder. He seemed to be deliberately trying to tease me as he cautiously removed the crating so he would not damage our treasure.

Finally, our radio stood, tall and gleaming, emitting a varnishy smell of newness in our sparsely furnished living room. Its resonance, although punctuated by frequent static and crane-like whoops, opened vast vistas of entertainment and imagination, just as the salesman had promised. Our Golden Age had truly begun!

Young people today are as conditioned to the presence of a radio as they are to an unending supply of shampoo. A radio, likely in the form of an I-Pod, is an appendage to their being whether they are driving, jogging, or ambling in and out of stores in the mall. To actually listen to a given program is rare. Often they ask, "But what did you look at while you listened to the radio?" ("Back in the olden days," they usually add.)

I always receive incredulous stares of curious sympathy when I tell them that I knew every sleazy gold and brown rayon thread of the fabric that covered our Philco's speaker. Those threads would dissolve into a jungle where Tarzan daily saved Jane, an athletic field where Jack Armstrong performed his All-American feats, or a gothic mansion where only the Shadow knew what evil lurked in the hearts of men. I had no doubt in my mind exactly what they all looked like.

The first winter that our Philco became a member of our family, I had a chance to share with my mother the glories of Soap Opera Heaven. Schools were closed due to a lengthy epidemic of scarlet fever and measles, and, as my measles spots faded, I was finally permitted to emerge from a green-shade-darkened room. While we sloshed grapefruit juice over crushed ice, Mom and I reveled in the pitfalls and passions of *Pepper Young's Family*, *The Romance of Helen Trent*, and the inimitable wisdom of *Ma Perkins*. True, we couldn't see all these beautiful people, but our imaginations worked overtime. Mom was sure Helen Trent would never snare that worthless Gil; I was equally sure that "fifteen years can make a difference," and that he'd dump her some day. Ma Perkins brought tears to our eyes daily with her eternal patience and goodness.

During the Oxydol commercials, Mom would hop up to crush more ice (pounding it in a cloth sugar sack with a tack hammer). By the time she found the bottom of her darning basket and her silk stockings looked like Swedish embroidery, I would grow tired of imagining. We'd set up a jigsaw puzzle or deal the cards for 500—both great Depression-time favorites—but we'd go right on listening to all of our friends. We could still see them in our minds' eyes.

When Dad came home, the last strains of Orphan Annie's theme were fading, and I'd copied the address given for the Ovaltine special offer for a post card picture of Annie and Sandy. Then the radio was all Dad's. Usually, I'd set the table rather than endure Amos and Andy. I could never understand them, let alone know what was so funny, but Dad always chuckled and slapped his knee while the unseen audience roared with the static.

Then Dad would "serious up" and get that tight look around his mouth while he listened to Lowell Thomas give the news. By then, Mom usually came in and perched on the arm of her chair like a worried-looking bird. I heard a lot about "Mussolini" in those days and thought it sounded like a recipe out of one of Mom's cookbooks. Usually I'd get through the news by lying on the floor and running my finger around the dime-sized hole my dog Tippy had chewed in the rug just before she died. The vegetable soup smell from the kitchen was powerful, and I kept thinking of the extra bowl of chocolate pudding I'd seen in the refrigerator. I waited, churning inside with impatience, for Lowell's inevitable, "So long until tomorrow."

After dinner (for we turned the radio off before dinner as devoutly as we asked the blessing), life with a sit-around radio was about what you may remember from *The Waltons*. Dad decided what the family would hear, and, believe me, there were no spare radios lurking in bedrooms to entertain dissatisfied children. If there were no programs my father pronounced worthwhile, he would resort to fiddling with the unfathomable "Mysteries of the Shortwave Band."

To me this meant you flipped a lever from the green band to a red band; and the glorious radio would emit teeth-edging shrieks and whistle threateningly. Occasionally, my father's face would light up as if he'd seen the Holy Grail. "Listen to that," he'd cry triumphantly. "I've got Warsaw!" Or Berlin. Or London. I had to take his word for it. All I knew was the people in those places talked funnier than Amos and Andy.

There was one distinctive voice in those days that became as familiar as Jack Benny's or Charlie McCarthy's, so much so that I came to visualize its owner as somewhat akin to God. To be told emphatically at age seven that the "only thing we have to fee-ah is fee-ah itself" is ominously inspiring, especially when shells are raining in Spain and you've learned Mussolini isn't a dessert.

A few years later that same voice would proclaim to my Monday morning social studies class that what had started out to be a placid, stodgy Sunday afternoon the day before was a day "that would live in infamy." We girls had sniffed fearfully, and the boys had gone right on drawing pictures of "dog fights." But the planes that fought were American and Japanese now, not Messerschmitts and the RAF.

Maybe FDR's words seemed the more prophetic and awesome since we couldn't trace the creases in his jowls or criticize him for five o'clock shadow. So, too, Tarzan's unseen jungle perhaps evoked an aura of mystery that even cinematography cannot capture. If our realm of experience didn't encompass California, we could easily picture *One Man's Family* living in a Midwestern farmhouse.

In other words, we didn't have everything delivered to us enclosed in vibrant, dizzying animation accompanied by multi-track stereo. Presidential election nights were times of interminable excitement. Baseball games had to be listened to diligently, for there were no instant replays. Entertainers became revered for their talent—not for their clothes or their sex appeal. Can you imagine Madonna having made it only on radio? Or Paris Hilton? How ironic if the inventive spirit that spawned the TV industry is now prepackaging all experience to the point of obliterating the very urge for creativity in our souls. Children sprawl, glazed-eyed and impassive, before a screen depicting every conceivable wonder—or horror. Voters return from the polls to learn that the Almighty Tube has already declared a winner. So why stand in line to vote, they ask. Last year's American Idol pick is forgotten or last year's favorite Desperate Housewife becomes this year's has-been as the medium produces a new, leggier, lashier version.

In the Golden Days of Radio, people and places seemed permanent in a world that was gearing up for astronomical change. In today's kaleidoscopic TV and computer-driven world, nothing seems permanent but everlasting, overwhelming change. The viewer spins in mindless confusion and monumental boredom.

Quo vadis, media?

The Golden Age of Radio previously appeared in *Good Old Days* and *Electric Consumer*.

OLD CLIFTY INN REVISITED

Like the Grand Dame of the valley, old Clifty Inn once stood, white-pillared and proud, more than four hundred feet above the Ohio River near Madison, Indiana. From the steamboat weathervane on her cupola to her stout, native stone foundation, the state park inn, built in 1924, beckoned as a haven for the work-weary during World War II.

Bound by dictates of gas rationing, visitors from the Indianapolis, Louisville, and Cincinnati areas vied for Clifty Inn's forty-six modest rooms with prices to match. Operated on the American plan, the Inn offered rooms with hot and cold running water (showers on each floor) and three heaped-up, family-style meals for a daily rate of $3.75 per person—a blockbuster bargain when 1944's average hourly wage in America was less than a dollar.

They came as families, they came as honeymooners, they came in groups of singles—mostly women, co-workers in war plants or offices—for weekend or weeklong respites from routine and rigors of whatever burdens the wartime world was placing on them. They were not disappointed.

Soft honeysuckle-laden air and cheery greetings from cardinals and mockingbirds greeted visitors as they pulled up to the Inn's front door. When they stepped through the lobby's French doors onto the porch, guests beheld a twelve-mile, heart-stopping panorama below: the Ohio River, a wide, shimmering ribbon, looping through a patchwork of fields, the sculptured, blue-gray Kentucky hills beyond, a river tug laboring behind barges loaded with steel or a Navy LST. A dime for the telescope captured up-close farmers working the fertile loam of the bottom lands—or rebuilding from last spring's capricious floods. To the west, the river took a glorious sweeping curve. The toy-like town of Madison lay to the east, its steeples and Federal-style buildings propped against a dense backdrop of wooded hills. At night Madison glistened like a collection of spilled jewels as the moon poured a path of molten silver across the Ohio. Only crickets or the lonely hoot of an owl broke the silence—or a riverboat's steady thumping—a reminder that war was blasting away, and that river traffic, vital to defending America, went on around the clock.

For all its natural ambiance, Clifty Inn offered far fewer comforts than today's budget-priced hotels. Yet clean rooms (no air conditioning, phones, or wall-to-wall carpets), comfortable beds and those three Herculean, all-you-can-eat meals a day kept guests content.

When it opened, Clifty Inn was hailed as being built on easily the most magnificent hotel site in the state. "The vistas are superb and the panoramas not excelled in the Rockies," said the Madison *Courier*. Madison residents surely believed in the Inn's future; they contributed $30,000 of the $75,000 cost to build the original thirty-two room building. In anticipation of the hundreds who would flock to the Inn for Sunday dinners, the dining room on the lower floor facing the river seated 250 persons. So popular did the Inn become after it opened in August, 1924, that a third story of fourteen rooms was added only three years later at a cost of $20,000. The number of visitors continued to climb throughout the 1930s.

When World War II began, gas rationing had a peculiar effect upon Clifty Inn's clientele. Located only 45 miles from Louisville, 72 miles from Cincinnati, and 86 miles from Indianapolis (those distances were before Interstates), Clifty triumphed as a just-right distance for weekend visitors and week-long vacationers. Reservations were at capacity in the summer months and for weekends in the spring and fall.

Midway through the war came Joe McDonald to take the manager's helm at Clifty Inn. Formerly operator of men's dormitories at Indiana University, McDonald had grown up on a 400-acre northern Indiana farm where he learned about ravenous appetites and mass meals from watching his mother and older sister Alice cook for hired hands. (Alice McDonald Nelson also made feeding people a career. She was Director of Housing at Indiana University for forty-five years.)

As he had at the IU dorms, Joe McDonald set a bountiful table for his guests, despite rationing and shortages. But first he revamped the Inn's antiquated kitchen. For nearly twenty years, back-wearying, coal-fired cook stoves had been the mainstay of Clifty's kitchen. Alma Demaree Hall, who joined the Clifty staff as a teenager in 1924, remembers the coal bin in the corner of the kitchen. "When the stove needed more coal, the person going through the kitchen, no matter who, had to grab the scoop shovel and carry coal across the kitchen and fire the stove."

To make Hoosier fried chicken his house specialty, McDonald chucked those coal-fired cook stoves, replacing them with cost-efficient electric ranges. He began serving crunchy, deep-fried chicken before Colonel Sanders ever put on a string tie. Not everyone was delighted with that crispiness, however. "It didn't taste southern enough," remembered Thelma McDonald, the managers' wife. "Joe and the cooks kept experimenting with how to use the efficiency of the deep fryer and still get the taste everyone wanted. They finally hit upon steaming it just a bit after it came out of the fryer. They'd place it in shallow pans and put hot, damp cloths over it to soften the outside until it tasted like 'what Grandma used to make.'"

Tuesday, Wednesday, and Thursday nights and Sunday afternoons until four o'clock, full-course fried chicken dinners with mountains of real whipped potatoes, fresh garden vegetables and salads, flaky, home-made yeast rolls and melt-in-your-mouth pies delighted guests of the sold-out Inn and more than one thousand drive-in diners during peak summer weeks.

Though guests took for granted the endless supply of chicken that smiling waitresses brought to their linen-covered tables, little did they know its history. Joe McDonald and his right-hand man, Oscar Humphreys, rattled around all week on the serpentine roads of southern Indiana and northern Kentucky in Clifty's 1939 Dodge panel truck to find those chickens. Since meat was rationed, chickens were in great demand. McDonald and Humphreys would race around barnyards to help obliging farmers round up the chickens for the kill. In a few hours the Dodge truck would chug into Madison to the local poultry house where the cargo would be dressed out and readied for the deep fryer. Dinner for drive-ins, or transients, was all of $1.50 in the 1940s, and family-style meant just that; like family, guests were welcome to have their chicken platters, vegetable and gravy bowls refilled.

How could Clifty Inn do this for a mere $1.50? "Volume is the key," McDonald always said. He kept close tabs on room and dinner reservations to be sure the Inn operated at capacity in the summer. During the off season, he encouraged traveling salesmen, holiday parties, college weekends, and high school proms. In an era before manufacturing plants had cafeterias, Clifty personnel catered company-paid holiday meals for employees at local factories. The Madison Rotary Club made Clifty Inn its headquarters for Thursday night dinner meetings all year long. All sorts of groups found their way to Clifty Inn in the off-season: from a top-echelon gathering of the Salvation Army, whose members touched everyone with their winsome spirit, to an unchaperoned Senior Class "Howl" from [the former] Western College for Women at Oxford, Ohio. McDonald afterward wrote Western's dean. "The young ladies were as gracious and charming as queens."

Alma Hall remembered the groups of tobacco buyers who wanted their seasoned ham dinners. "After scrubbing the mold off those big old aged hams," she said, "we had to boil them, then bake them in whiskey, but they were truly wonderful. Unfortunately, sometimes the men got roasted in whiskey, too."

If the Inn offered a family atmosphere, it was partly because a family operated it. To be sure, McDonald, his wife Thelma and their children—one a teenager and one a toddler—made their home at the Inn. But "The Macs" treated the entire staff as a close-knit family who had genuine concern for its guests.

"He (McDonald) was such a genial host, and he did everything to make our stays enjoyable," said Stella Koch of Cincinnati. Ms. Koch and the Blue Grass Square Dance Club, went to Clifty Inn for more than ten years for weekends in May as well as on the Fourth of July and Labor Day weekend. She called square dances on Saturday nights outdoors on the tennis courts or indoors in the cleared-out dining room if the weather was inclement.

Ms. Koch, when still active as a travel agent at age 84, said, "I can smell that Sunday fried chicken right now. And what great friends we made of members of the staff and the other folks from around the area who came to enjoy Clifty's hospitality. There were such special people, like Mildred (Shorty) Spotts, the dining room hostess, whose gracious ways were remembered by guests from one year to the next."

Retired minister E. Dean Finley of Greencastle, Indiana, recalls fond memories of summers spent as a naturalist at Clifty Inn when he was a college student. "It was always a treat to hold song fests and slide lectures out on that marvelous porch." Finley recalled making good friends with the waitresses in the dining room and once even going so far as to intercede with Mr. McDonald on their behalf. The issue was wages, which the girls felt were inadequate. "Unfortunately," Finley said, "I was not mature enough to know I should not get involved. Mr. McDonald was not pleased with my interference, I vividly remember. He let me know how such matters were not my concern. It was a good lesson for me to learn. He was very kind to me, though, and probably more tolerant of my foibles than he should have been."

A number of full-time employees lived nearby in "The Cottage," men on the first floor, women on the second. Day rooms offered part-time workers a place to rest between the noon and evening meals. There were no posted rules, no closing hours, no locks on doors. If there was an unofficial house mother, it was head cook Frances Ringwald. Ringie listened to confidences, moderated squabbles and dispensed enough homespun wisdom to fill a dozen advice books. When she'd run up against a particular knotty problem, she'd wag her head, push her square-rimmed glasses up on her nose, smiling all the while, saying, "Mother always said there'd be days like this."

"They [the cooks] were like our mothers at work," said Ruth Ann (Sauley) Demaree. Along with three classmates, Ruth Ann waited tables weekends and summer months throughout high school. "When we came in from our dates, there was always 'Goodnight, girls,' from their rooms at the top of the stairs. They checked to be sure we did our homework and were always there for us if we needed someone to talk to. Mr. Mac [McDonald] kept close watch on us, too, yet he was very nice to all of us."

Although employees enjoyed a liberated living atmosphere, they endured a strict dress code while on duty. Waitresses and cooks not only wore spotless uniforms but also (though grudgingly) donned hairnets and headbands. Desk clerks and bellhops dared not appear without sport coats, dress shirts and pants, and ties. Shoes, real shoes not sneakers, demanded daily polishing. Along with dressing for the job, courteous treatment of guests was imperative. "Yes, ma'ams" and "No, sirs," came as naturally as chicken and biscuits, and no reasonable request by a guest was ever ignored. What Clifty's accommodations lacked in luxury, the ample meals and down-home service made up for.

For entertainment, visitors to Clifty Inn found themselves surrounded by 350 acres of undefiled woods, natural wildlife, crystal-clean air, and miles of well-marked trails to hike or ride on horses rented at the park stables. In the 1930s, Indiana state parks had reaped ample benefits from the New Deal's Civilian Conservation Corps (CCC). Hundreds of unemployed young men from cities had built roads and trails and shelters, gate houses and stables, putting the Hoosier state's park facilities far ahead of many surrounding states at that time.

An unscheduled inspection visit to a camp for CCC workers located in Clifty Falls State Park brought the Inn's most distinguished visitor. In 1934, Mrs. Eleanor Roosevelt, traveling with two companions, Mrs. Marian Dickerman and Miss Nancy Cook of Hyde Park, New York, drove her sports model roadster through Indiana without a Secret Serviceman in sight. Alma Hall remembered Mrs. Roosevelt very well. Although Hall did not wait on the First Lady, she sat at a table next to one Alma Hall was serving. "She was dressed very plainly," Hall said, "in a white lawn summer dress with a little lace at the neck and white cotton hose and plain white tennis shoes. Not what I called a pretty woman, but charming, and talked to all of us girls, which was a thrill in our young lives."

Mrs. Roosevelt, the Madison *Courier* reported, sat on the Inn's veranda and observed the scenery with binoculars for some time before touring the park and the CCC camp. She praised the beauty of the hotel's site and expressed a desire to return in the future. A newspaper photo of the Inn marked the room the First Lady occupied on the third floor, southwest corner. There was no elevator or even a private bath—just the Inn's best view of the broad river's sweeping curve and a panorama of hills.

A naturalist, employed by the State Department of Conservation, joined the staff each summer to lead guests on rugged or non-rugged hikes, auto trips to surrounding points of interest, song fests, Bingo games, and nature slide-shows. Miss Iva Spangler, a high school biology teacher from Ft. Wayne, filled the naturalist's job during the first couple of years of the war. Wearing her twill jodhpurs, knee-high boots, and a grosgrain hair ribbon, she'd grab her walking stick, sling her binoculars around her neck and lead her charges with twice the stamina of the most eager hikers in her group. Younger staff members soon affectionately, though secretly, nicknamed her "Tweets and Twitters." When a bus boy slipped one day and addressed her as "Tweets," she looked puzzled for a moment. Then her cornflower-blue eyes crinkled and her bridgework sparkled. "I didn't know bus boys could talk like birds," she said and calmly went on eating her pie.

If children attempted too-long hikes or an occasional guest was a blatant know-it-all about fields of her expertise, Miss Spangler's patience and low-key sense of humor would come to her rescue. A singer she was not, but she was game enough to lead evening song fests on the porch. Relying on her trusty pitch pipe, she'd labor through now-taboo favorites like "In the Evening by the Moonlight" and "Old Black Joe." If the crowd was listless, they'd find themselves working off their dinners by hopping up and down to sing "Today is Monday" and the "Teensy-Weensy Spider."

When there were no scheduled activities, canasta players crowded the lobby's hickory chairs and tables, day and night. Sometimes a piano player appeared, and spirited, impromptu sing-a-longs and the "Old Kentucky Homes" would try to out-sing the "Back Home Again in Indianas."

A Philco console radio with a manual turntable on top and a scratchy collection of 78s offered the only other entertainment. But some people can remember hearing about the bombing of Hiroshima on that radio. And some can still imagine themselves dancing there with the heady perfume of honeysuckle drifting through the open French doors every time they hear Glenn Miller's "Moonlight Serenade."

A small gift shop adjoining the lobby offered a mish-mash of key chains, letter openers, and ceramic state birds as well as some nicer pieces. One of the most popular was a Staffordshire plate, imported for Clifty Inn from England and bearing a color image of the Inn from its proud river side. Since only a limited number of these plates were imported, any in existence are sure to be of some value to collectors today. (see photo p. 60.)

The gift shop's proprietor often played canasta with guests in the lobby but sat where he could eyeball his prospects through a glass wall lined with knick-knack laden shelves. Known as Grandad by everyone, twice-widowed J. Newton Clements was Thelma McDonald's father, retired but seldom idle. Clifty secretary Jean Dunn Yager recalls catching him dozing one time, though. On a wild impulse, she perched her lace-trimmed hanky on his bald head. When he woke up, he bristled at the idea of how foolish he'd looked but leaped to his feet to serve his prospective customers. A slight, wiry but determined man, Grandad would suddenly bolt from the card table, muttering something, "I'm gonna sell that sucker that china hand. She can't resist it since I told her yesterday it was modeled off the hand of the Empress Josephine." Grandad, a true disciple of P.T. Barnum, did a brisk business.

Grandad also proudly claimed he'd voted for every Republican since McKinley. At that time, Indiana's Governor Henry F. Schricker—of the opposite political party—was known by his oversized white Stetson hat. While attending a luncheon at Clifty Inn one day, the governor placed his famed Stetson on a hat rack in the lobby alongside dozens of more ordinary headgear. No one was ever sure whose idea it was: a canasta player, gift shop customer, or an idle bellboy who challenged, "Why don't you try on Governor Schricker's hat, Grandad? See if it turns color on a Republican like you."

"Nah…I wouldn't put on that geek's hat." One hand unconsciously smoothed his bald pate as he fanned out his cards in the other.

Other voices chimed in. "C'mon…" "I'll take your picture." "You're not chicken, are you, Grandad?"

Slamming down his cards, Grandad ground out his Camel in the brimming ashtray. "I'll show you birds…get that camera." The famous hat already in hand, he bounded out the door and across the driveway to the stone steps, a favorite picture-taking backdrop, where his audacity would be recorded for the ages.

Another lively gentleman sparked the surroundings. Guests would sometimes be startled to hear a vaudeville-style rendition of "Puttin' on the Ritz" or "Sweet Sue" burst forth from behind the reservation desk. John Byam, former song-and-dance man, claimed he'd played to houses where Fred Astaire and the Castles (Vernon and Irene) performed. Byam appeared from nowhere and worked at the Inn's front desk for more than ten years. He would also do a bit of soft shoe at the slightest provocation and could spin an instant story from his show-biz past. He was a caring person who would empathize with guests' dilemmas and do his best to satisfy their whims. Lithe and vigorous with a personality to match, yet he was a very private person who kept to himself during his off hours, steering clear of social entanglements. He made many female hearts flutter though. It was wartime and single men of eligible age were not spending their days and nights at Clifty Inn. Eventually, Byam left Clifty Inn in the 1950s and tended the front desk at a nearby Madison hotel. There he gained fleeting fame, even *Time* magazine coverage, by tangling with a raucous and dissatisfied customer—Frank Sinatra. Sinatra, Dean Martin, and Shirley MacLaine were in town for the filming of *Some Came Running*.

Young Joey McDonald, the manager's son, went to live at the Inn when he was two years old. The Clifty staff became an extended family for him until he reached his teens and his father no longer managed the Inn. Joey had an imagination that ran full throttle, and most frequently he was Superman. Daily he'd fashion and decorate a cape from one of the Inn's guest towels. Father thought he put a stop to this, but bookkeeper Ruth Land was never too busy to secure Superman's cape with paper clips and give him a piece of candy besides. Then away Joey would go, leaping from stone walls or flinging himself out onto the porch to the dismay of guests who were enjoying the serenity of the river view. "Faster than the speed of light," he'd shout, as he'd head for the railing. But just as someone would reach out to grab the pesky kid, he'd shift roles. Flinging aside his cape, he'd suddenly begin building a "tank" out of two wicker ottomans. Firing away with imaginary weapons, Joey was off "chasing Japs."

One of Joey's special pals was desk clerk Frank Pritchard. A bachelor and former Madison mayor, Pritchard had also headed the Boys' Club of Madison. He spent many off-duty hours down on the bank of the Ohio, teaching little Joey to fish. "I don't remember we ever caught much," said McDonald, now a Carmel, Indiana resident. "But the lunches the cooks packed for us were tremendous. The milk that came out of that thermos was the coldest I ever tasted."

Pritchard became friend and confidante to the staff's young people. A certain two-seated maple settee in the lobby might well have had a sign over it saying, "The Doctor is In." Often during Pritchard's long night shift, an off-duty waitress or two, a bellhop or desk clerk would hunker down next to him, sharing plans for the future or getting help sorting through problems. They were good listeners, too, and from Pritchard young folks gained a perspective of what life had been like for him as mayor of their town during the dim, dark days of the Depression. As teenagers, they could but vaguely remember their parents speaking of hard times, for wartime had brought with it a booming prosperity. Pritchard helped give his young friends a clearer window on their world than their parents had time to do or their teachers had patience for.

Cars were having to "make-do" until after the war, and virtually no teenagers had cars of their own. Pritchard owned a 1941 Chrysler coupe, the last pre-war model. Aside from his fishing forays with Joey, he only drove it on Sunday evenings when he took his lady friend, Nora Schwab, to dinner at the Central Hotel. Afterwards they would attend whatever movie was playing at the Ohio Theater. While the manager's son has fond memories of fishing trips with Pritchard, the manager's daughter (the writer) remembers how generously he'd loan her that coupe when her parents' car was not available. A pattern developed.

"Frankie-doodle," she'd say, "what's new?" Before the question was out, Pritchard was reaching for his car keys, steely blue eyes twinkling behind his rimless lenses. This was a mutual trust, by the way, never abused by on-the-impulse joyrides to Louisville or leaving Pritchard with an empty gas tank. Frank Pritchard's way of treating young people with respect and dignity made them feel a need to live up to his belief in them.

Bill Cranford and Bill Robinson worked at Clifty Inn throughout high school, first as bellhops, then desk clerks.

The summer after their graduation was no different except they were waiting to be drafted as soon as they turned eighteen. Time probably was dragging for them. To liven up the surroundings, this duo staged a daring practical joke. Hearing of an inmate's escape from nearby Madison State Hospital, the two devilish clerks hatched a plot to trick bellhop Charlie Chowning. Fourteen-year-old Charlie was as short on nerve as he was in stature.

"Hey, Charlie, did'ja hear on the radio about that knife maniac that escaped from the state hospital today?" Bill R. tried to act nonchalant as he breezed into work one afternoon. "Yeah, Charlie, he was sighted heading this way, toward the park." Bill C., getting ready to go off duty, turned away, trying not to smirk at the fright that paled Charlie's freckled face.

Pinpoints of fear jabbed Charlie's wide brown eyes. "L-l-l-et me know if you hear anything more," he stammered, scurrying off to fill the Coke machine.

The plot devised by the heartless Bills involved borrowing a chef's knife with a ten-inch blade from Alma Hall's salad table after the kitchen closed that evening. Bill C., disguised in frumpy clothes, hid, along with the knife he'd polished until it gleamed, in the honeysuckle at the end of the lane that led to the help's Cottage.

At eleven o'clock, Charlie asked Bill R. to wait while he straightened the lobby so they could walk to the Cottage together. Of course, Bill knew Charlie wouldn't want to walk the dark lane alone. All evening he'd kept asking if there was any new report about the escaped inmate. Each time Bill R. had invented some news flash—a bandana found on a tree in the park, bloodhounds on the escapee's trail, troops coming from Camp Atterbury to search the woods.

"I'm sure glad you've got a flashlight, Bill." Charlie's voice sounded forced, as if someone had tied a muffler around his neck.

"The last report I heard," Bill said, "a park ranger said the police thought he might have gone down into the Clifty canyon to hide."

An owl hooted from a nearby tree. Charlie reached to grab Bill's arm. "Cut it out, Charlie. It's only a stupid owl. When are you going to grow up anyway?"

At the sound of their voices, an unrecognizable, bedraggled Bill C. leaped from the dense shrubbery, brandishing the knife and laughing fiendishly. Of course, Bill R.'s flashlight beam caught the full length of the shiny blade.

Charlie seemed to evaporate, his spine-shivering screams trailing behind him as he howled his way back to the Inn. The Bills had expected this and clued night clerk Frank Pritchard to their plan. Although he didn't approve, Pritchard agreed to console Charlie and explain the "joke."

The perpetrators had some explaining to do themselves. Heads began popping out of windows of the Inn.

"What's going on?" "Somebody call the police!" "I thought this place was supposed to be peaceful."

Bill Cranford took control. "Guess we'd better come up with something to quiet them down before Mr. Mac hears all this." Bill could usually come up with some sort of half-way believable tall tale in any situation.

Bill stood in the driveway and called up to the wild-eyed guests. "It's OK everyone. You can go back to sleep." "Everything's under control. A guy fell asleep in his car in the parking lot. Guess he had a nightmare and couldn't figure out where he was." Voices rumbled, lights snapped off in the windows above. No sign of Mr. Mac.

Those Bills had the personalities and gift of gab that could talk their way into and out of most anything. But the next morning, after they'd laughed most of the night over their uproarious stunt, the two young clerks were as humble and meek as choirboys.

Mr. McDonald deliberately kept them waiting a half hour before asking them to come into his private office. Standing, looking out the window with his back to them when they arrived, McDonald gave a clue to his mood. "Don't bother sitting down," he said. His tone was flat.

The Bills looked at each other wordlessly. Was he really going to sack them over a stupid prank?

Finally, Mr. Mac turned around, his glasses fogged up and his brown eyes brimming. He was laughing! "Try as I want to, I can't get all that mad at you two clowns for what I heard about this morning. You sure must have scared the pants off that kid. It was a heartless way to do it, but maybe you helped him to grow up a bit."

Stealing a glance at each other and trying not to smile, the Bills thought they were home free. Wrong. Mr. Mac raised his voice. "Now get out there on that porch while the guests are at breakfast and use some muscle instead of those devious brains of yours. Give it a good hosing down and then wash every one of the panes on all four pairs of French doors, inside and out! And let me know when you've finished. I'll decide then if there are other things for you to do this morning."

Although not used to doing such menial chores, the two Bills congratulated themselves for weeks for pulling off this stunt and

Tapestry

keeping their jobs. Charlie recovered and did, in fact, seem a little less fearful and gullible after that made-to-order, bone-chilling experience.

Several former employees recall Dr. Guy Hamilton, who made his home at Clifty Inn for a number of years. A psychiatrist and former medical missionary to China, Dr. Hamilton settled in at Clifty Inn during his retirement years. A gentleman and a scholar who spent his days reading and writing for medical journals, Dr. Hamilton's daily regimen included an eight-mile hike to Clifty Falls and back every morning after breakfast.

"Forced march is more like it," the manager's son Joey remembers. "My dog Laddie went with him nearly every day—and then would sleep all afternoon."

"Each morning," naturalist Dean Finley said, "Dr. Hamilton would be returning, perspiring profusely and red-faced, from a brisk eight-mile walk. I admired him very much. He could have walked or hiked circles around me, I'm sure."

Often, the doctor's son, Dr. Joseph Hamilton, and his family would drive up from Louisville and bring their two young daughters, Polly and Ellen, to have dinner with "Peepaw," the girls' nickname for their grandfather.

As with most children who came often to the Inn, Polly and Ellen became playmates of young Joey McDonald. "One of our favorite games," McDonald recalled, "was to roll in the sheets at the bottom of the clothes chute in the first-floor linen room." McDonald said he met Polly Hamilton at a party in Louisville years later when they were both in high school. She didn't care to be reminded of that particular pastime.

Jaunty Dr. Guy Hamilton, with his snow-white hair and mustache, his ruddy face, and impeccable manner impressed everyone with his gracious manner and his zest for living. You could be sure that in every conversation with Dr. Hamilton you would learn at least one new word or worthwhile fact. His command of language was as succinct as his mustache was neatly trimmed.

Upon her graduation from Hanover College, the author received "a little yellow slip of paper" (a check) from the good doctor who had encouraged her throughout her college years. "I wish this were more commensurate with the dignity and importance of the day," he wrote, "but be assured it carries a load of congratulations and good wishes for the future which extends so invitingly before you." This proper yet sincere typewritten note signed by Guy W. Hamilton has been in the receiver's scrapbook for more than fifty years, a treasured memory of a sincere and dignified gentleman.

Though there was nothing architecturally significant about old Clifty Inn, and its accommodations were anything but luxurious, a certain aura existed there during the war years. Perhaps it summed up what America was all about—what our troops were dying for in remote places with strange-sounding names—Guadalcanal, Iwo Jima, Anzio, Tunisia. Friends and families gathered around bountiful tables—the pristine natural setting far above a majestic river—simple entertainments and pleasures—people who cared about one another and worked happily together to make their guests' brief vacations as meaningful and enjoyable as possible.

Note: Struck by a vicious tornado in 1974, old Clifty Inn stood roofless and abandoned for several years. Restoring it was finally deemed impractical, and a rambling contemporary structure has replaced it. Vintage photos of the old Clifty Inn hang in the lobby, nostalgic reminders of the past.

Reprinted from *Showers of Blessings: A Journal of Ohio Valley Life* © 1993 Patricia McDonald Mote. Quixote Publications.

Clifty Inn in the 1940s

Clifty Inn after the 1974 tornado

DECEMBER AFTERNOON

A gloomy Sunday afternoon in early December can be the deadliest time of the week when you're three weeks away from your eleventh birthday. There's no one under 35 at home in the neighborhood, and Mom is swamped with the demands of my baby brother. Too old for the draft, Dad has taken a job at an Army post several hundred miles away—to do his bit for the "war effort." I keep hearing that phrase though the "war" is only happening in those pink and green blobs my teacher points to on the map of Europe.

Mom settles down to listen to a church service on the radio, so I figure she'll let me spend some of my 25-cent weekly allowance on a Sunday afternoon movie. I'm glad I went to Sunday School, or she'd never let me go to the movies.

Soon I'm on my way, walking, for my bike has a flat waiting for Dad to fix when he comes home next weekend. I cut through the college campus, the shortest way to the downtown theater. In this small Indiana town in 1941, rapes and muggings are unknown. I trust every inch of the wooded campus. Each ivy-covered building is a trusted friend.

I pay a dime admission to see Abbott and Costello in *Hold That Ghost,* another dime for some Milk Duds and look for a seat near the back. I don't want to sit near other kids who'd think I'm weird, going to a show alone. But anything is better than staying home and being lonely. I wish I could see *The Wizard of Oz* again: Abbott and Costello sometimes are pretty dumb.

In the newsreel, Hitler's storm troopers are goose-stepping through the streets of Berlin. A short figure with a mustache stands stiffly on a balcony. Soldiers' heads snap to the right. Saluting, they shout the now-familiar, "Sieg heil!" I giggle, trying to picture troops strutting by the Capitol in Washington. Would the president give them a jaunty wave with that long cigarette holder of his?

When the screen suddenly gets dark, I suppose something is wrong in the projection booth. But the house lights come on, and the manager steps in front of the curtain: "Ladies and gentlemen," his voice is solemn and shakes a little, "This morning the Japanese attacked the American naval base at Pearl Harbor in Hawaii. American losses are believed to be heavy." His voice is shaky. A few people gasp, a woman's scream of "War!" pierces the theater.

Everyone sits frozen in shock as the movie comes back on. Then, as if the darkness is a cue, somber lines of movie-goers snake silently toward the exits. The cartoon is on now, and Mickey Mouse squawks to an emptying theater.

Outside, I expect things to look or seem different somehow. But there are no sirens, no sounds of approaching planes. Instead, noisy college students crowd into an ice cream store. Sam, the hot tamale vendor, works his customary corner. Christmas carols float past from the manger scene on the courthouse lawn.

A bus clatters by while I'm waiting for a traffic light. I'd love to climb aboard to a quicker route to home and safety. But I remember the Milk Duds and that I have only five cents left.

Running now, panting, half-sobbing, I cover the 12 blocks to home. This time I avoid the quiet woods and follow streets that border the campus. I don't want to be alone in the leaden, dismal afternoon.

Glancing up, I assure myself no Japanese bombers are diving through the gray-flannel sky. A truck backfires, and I scurry behind a huge oak and hug its gnarled, solid trunk. Will anything ever seem safe and sure again?

Though the war never physically touched me, things never really were the same again. Selling War Stamps and collecting tin cans with the Girl Scouts and having only one pair of shoes a year were my contacts with the war.

Three-and-a-half years later my friends and I snake-danced around a huge bonfire to celebrate the end of this war I had never really felt. But my boyfriend sobbed that night while the crowd shouted and sang "God Bless America." His brother had died on Guadalcanal.

Though scars have healed, the vibrations of that war have shaken my life ever since. My husband and I now own a Japanese car, and last year we took a long-saved-for vacation in Germany. But I've lived with a grim, gnawing memory of that same fear ever since that December day in 1941. And our generation raised our children under a mushroom cloud of fear.

Today, and tomorrow, I struggle to cope with the frantic pace of choices and changes that war initiated. I continue to pray that the valiant determination that existed in the 1940s survives today. I pray, too, that such courage will be tempered with a global vision, a universal altruism, and an unwavering faith in humanity's ability to discover how to survive extinction.

I affirm the faith of author William Faulkner when he said, "I believe that man will not merely endure; he will prevail. . . . I decline to accept the end of man."

December Afternoon previously appeared under various titles in the *Cincinnati Enquirer Magazine*, The Columbus (IN) *Republic*, and the Cleveland *Plain Dealer*.

HONORS DAY: 1968

A somber, pewter sky had dumped a before-dawn cloudburst on the downtown streets, and by 8:45 a.m. a late spring thunderstorm threatened. The locust trees that marched around Central Junior High School in full leaf this June morning drooped with heavy wetness.

I stood next to Principal Lee Leonard near the gym entrance, watching hundreds of students pour out of the main building, weaving a solid band of life and color as they came across rain-swept Pearl Street. Honors Day Convocation was a milestone in Central's school year, and since I didn't have a homeroom, I was assigned to help with general supervision.

Mr. Leonard smiled and nodded to teachers and students, stooping to rough up the curly hair of an undersized seventh grade boy. Although not an outgoing man by nature, Lee Leonard was a shrewd observer of people, always in tune with this school. This morning he was trying, I could tell, to assess the mood of his student body. I was worried about the length of the convocation. The seventh graders, especially, would get fidgety. Still, Mr. Leonard had resisted suggestions to shorten the program. He remained adamant that Central Junior High would recognize achievement—whether for academics, athletics, perfect attendance or flag-raising.

As I searched faces for mood cues this rainy June morning, I could tell most students had not heard early-morning news flashes. (This was before the era of cable news and teenagers with headphone implants.)

Funneling through the gym doors, the students looked much as they did on any other school day—except the ninth graders, who were a little more dressed up. This was their farewell to Central. In this small conservative community, there was still a dress code in 1968. Girls' skirts were shorter, admittedly, but they were still wearing skirts to school. And bras, too. Boys' tee-shirts boasted only names of schools or teams, not breweries or rock stars, and Beatle-bangs were the nearest thing to long hair for boys. School policy still dictated, "Above the ears and above the collar."

Inside the gym, humidity hung like a dense curtain, the air ripe with imbedded sweat of decades of battles on the basketball courts. At the top of the bleachers, custodian Harley Jackson opened more windows trying to relieve the oppressive atmosphere. Steel-guarded ceiling lights, like eerie white eyes, bore down on the colorful scene below.

Blue-robed ninth grade chorus members mounted risers on the gym floor. The girls teetered in unaccustomed high heels, while the boys, twisting their necks like young cranes, chafed against unwelcome white shirts and ties. A curious mixture of Heaven-Scent and bubblegum mingled with the sweat-laden air.

Students were filling both bleachers and the balcony now. Every moment, the level of student noise seemed to rise a few more decibels. Band members began tuning their instruments as the PA system shrieked a final check.

Eying the clock on the west wall, Mr. Leonard gave a nod to Steve Spencer, Student Council president. Only one-and-one-half minutes late, I noted, my mind spanning the continent in a second. What time is it now in California?

Suddenly, what seemed to be thunder was actually the student body rising for the Pledge of Allegiance. With no directions, 1,300-plus young people took their cue from their president as he mounted the stage and faced the American flag. Central students know about loyalty and respect, I thought grimly, no matter what's going on in the rest of the country.

Following the National Anthem, Mary Munson stepped briskly to her podium. In her first year as Central's vocal music director, this was her first Honors Day. She raised her baton and fifty-two young voices began—

To dream...the impossible dream

To fight...the unbeatable foe...

To bear with unbearable sorrow...

To run...where the brave dare not go... The chorus sang with such precision and earnestness that ninth grade girls were fumbling in their purses for tissues, and seventh grade boys had stopped wiggling.

That one man, scorned and covered with scars,

Still strove with his last ounce of courage,

To reach...the unreachable star...

The final chord hung suspended like a glowing, invisible presence.

Now Steve was introducing Ben Bartlett, the athletic director, who would announce the awards. The squares of half-light showing through the windows were growing feebler. When a branch scraped a window as the wind rose, I tried not to think of tornadoes. Someone in the clarinet section knocked over a music stand, prompting a brief eruption of giggles.

"The words of this song describe the quest, the search, of a very famous man," Ben began. "Although not a real person, his compelling story was told hundreds of years ago by a Spaniard. The legendary tale of Don Quixote has affected the entire world."

Ben's voice filled all corners of the gym as the students listened intently. In a few well-chosen statements, he drew a graphic, verbal portrait of the determined, would-be knight and his quest for a better world.

"When I saw the program for today, my first thought was to talk about striving, searching, never giving up—as Don Quixote felt he must act, how we must all do this. Of course, I'd have talked some about striving on the football field." He flashed a grin." I'd have undoubtedly told you one more time about losing at the Rose Bowl not all that many years ago when I was a student myself—but how we never stopped trying." There were some spatterings of applause, then abrupt silence.

"This morning we're here to honor those Central students who have achieved this year in a number of ways. They've brought honor to themselves to their families, and to our school. They have followed their stars to achieve excellence in many different ways. For some, they may have gained what they felt was the unreachable star.

"But first, we must, sadly, pay tribute to another fine American whose life has been canceled out by an assassin's bullet." A tense hum of student voices rose. Ben continued, and the voices dropped away.

"Robert Kennedy died from an assassin's bullet early this morning in Los Angeles." A muted murmur of voices swelled again.

Ben chose his words carefully. He spoke reverently of Bobby Kennedy's ideal world in which compassion for one's fellow man would be a motivating factor for mankind. His voice cracked with emotion, his words washed over me like a rushing tide. "Somehow to carry on… others who will follow…so that his ideals will be realized…"

I glanced over at my principal, still standing next to me. His bright blue eyes were glassy, fixed straight ahead, his jaw squared. Ben was closing his remarks with words the chorus had just sung:

And I know if I'll only be true, to this glorious quest

That my heart will lie peaceful and calm

When I'm laid to my rest...

And the world will be better for this:

That one man, scorned and covered with scars,

Still strove, with his last ounce of courage,

To reach...the unreachable star...

Ben spoke the final words as if they were a benediction.

Unashamed of the bitter tears stinging my cheeks, I thought of a poster hanging in my classroom; a student had made it only last week—Bobby Kennedy's words from his speech just two months ago in Indianapolis: "What we need in this world is more love and compassion toward one another." Would those words ring hollow for my students now?

"He made our world better. That's what our preacher said about Dr. King," Steve Spencer had said after King was shot only two months before. "Do people have to get shot for their dreams to come true? Or will they ever anyway—with all the kooks in the world?"

My eyes swept the bleachers on either side. How many of these young people were remembering a gray November day when their second or third or fourth grade teacher told them that the President of their country had been shot and killed? For five years, that day and the tragic ones that followed have been a blurred vision in their consciousness. Now in the glory and promise of springtime, America has sacrificed two more valiant men whose lives stood for goodness and compassion.

Band members raised their instruments, and the strains of Central's "Alma Mater" leaped toward the steel rafters. Young, vibrant voices had regained their poise to sing of loyalty and truth. "The Hope of Our Country," I thought, just as it's carved in stone over the side entrances of our school. But I wondered in how many other American schools today ceremonies of honor are being played out against an incongruous background of assassination and hatred.

I looked again at faces for signs of disillusionment, even bitterness, that I knew were growing in some young hearts. Outwardly, and for the moment at least, they seemed intent upon singing their praises and devotion to their school. But for how long?

Now the eighth and ninth grade baseball teams were queuing up to accept their letters and certificates. A burst of lightning filled the square windows above the bleachers, followed by a roof-bumping rumble of thunder.

The storm was sure to hit soon.

Lyrics from "The Impossible Dream" from *The Man of LaMancha* (New York: Sam Fox Publishing, 1965).

FLAGS, RIBBONS, AND A ROOT CANAL

Squirming in the dentist's chair, inwardly at least, I waited, growing number by the minute. Having a root canal was not my idea of how to spend a rare sunny day in February.

Through the window I could see an American flag flinging itself out over Pearl Road. At its base was an orange ribbon. Seeing flags on every lamp post along the street made me feel as if I should see a parade turning the corner and coming toward me.

Just then, the dentist's assistant appeared at my side. A badge with orange ribbons peeped out from behind her mask that hung against her chest. "Till they all come home," the badge said.

Funny combination, these orange ribbons and Old Glory. Orange is not an unfamiliar color here in Browns' Country, perhaps, or downstate in Cincinnati Bengals' territory where it's said to have had its start. Maybe that lady who tied the first one on her porch used up some ribbons left over from a Bengals' party. Just think, if this idea had started in Houston, all of these ribbons might be Oilers' baby blue.

I shook my head at the assistant. No, I wasn't numb all the way yet. As if on cue with my thoughts about the flag, the badge, and the ribbons, I realized the radio was sending out Sandi Patti's rendition of "The Star Spangled Banner" complete with what sounded like at least six Navy bands. Even at the comforting dentist-office volume, Sandi does a stirring bit with the anthem, but this was the third time I'd heard it today. Good old media overkill.

The music kept me thinking about all of the flags and ribbons I'd seen already today. More flags than I remember in my entire town during World War II. Flags weren't mass produced cheaply then, and, besides, there were all kinds of fabric shortages. Women even painted on make-believe stockings. And certainly there were no colored flags to cut out of the newspapers.

The most common emblem people had then were the small star-in-the-window banners—blue stars in homes that had servicemen fighting, gold stars where a loved one had been killed in action. At a few homes an oversized American flag would hang between trees or from a flagpole. You knew where those had come from. But most families kept those flags sealed away, folded in their tight triangles, to give to a child whose father didn't come home.

Flags are only one evidence of a fervor pumping up the national psyche. Bumper stickers as well as badges proclaim our pride. Ribbons sprout from antennas and trees. Desert Storm tee-shirts congregate in store windows.

During World War II, Americans didn't yet have the habit of pasting their beliefs on their bumpers or advertising allegiances across their chests. Bumpers (at least front ones) were for pushing cars that had run out of the monthly gas ration, and tee-shirts were still—just underwear. But of Americans' dedication and involvement in the war effort there had been no doubt. Youngsters collected tin cans and made huge tinfoil balls to turn in for scrap, while their mothers worked in war plants, and their grandmothers knitted socks and rolled bandages. Grandfathers forgot about retiring.

If the present war continues and the lists of casualties in Operation Desert Storm grow longer, can Americans sustain this burgeoning show of pride in our troops and in our country's actions? Right now, even those who publicly disapprove of the war are carrying flags to show their respect and support for our fighting men and women. And rightly so. If it hadn't been for generations of soldiers—beginning with the Minutemen—how would these concerned citizens have the right to protest their government's actions? What will happen when we realize this war is not a miniseries or a video game that we can ignore if we don't like what's going on or if we tire of it? If our tee-shirts and our ribbons fade and our flags tatter, will we stash them aside and flaunt something else that doesn't depress us? With the mindset of instant gratification that is imbedded in our consciousness, do we have the staying power to uphold this mood of patriotism so long overdue in our country?

Let's trust that our flags and ribbons really mean support, loyalty and pride in our troops and our nation. But if they are just symbols of a follow-the-crowd euphoria, only to be discarded in rough going (like the 1990 Browns' buttons?), they'll become meaningless, empty shams.

"We're ready now. You'll do fine." My kind, gentle dentist's voice interrupted my thoughts. He gave me a reassuring smile before he ducked into his mask and rolled his chair next to mine.

I tried to smile back through the numbness. "Let's get going." I mumbled, giving him an OK sign.

It would be great, I thought, if I could watch that waving flag through the window to help me through this ordeal. After all, what's a root canal compared to a desert foxhole?

Flags, Ribbons and a Root Canal previously appeared in the Cleveland *Plain Dealer*.

PULSE OF A NATION

On January 20, 1993, I was one of thousands of Americans packed shoulder to shoulder in front of the U.S. Capitol. There, under a cloudless, cobalt-blue sky, in thirty-ish temperatures, a 46-year-old governor, his lawyer/wife, and their starry-eyed twelve-year-old daughter—owner of a cat named Socks—would become America's first family, at least for four years.

From our red-ticket vantage point near the reflecting pool, my friend and I stood for more than three hours, waiting for history to unroll. True, those at home had a better view on their TV screens. But nothing could compare with the emotions triggered by the incredible feeling of being a part of the history being made there that day.

Each ticket holder seemed to be allowed about a four-foot square. Once you cleared security, inched your way forward and staked your claim, there was no turning back. Forget refreshments or restrooms. The area surrounding us was to become a microcosm of our society for the next few hours. It was a youthful crowd, typical of the Clinton-Gore campaign. There was a light sprinkling of us plus-fifties and an equally light sprinkling of minorities.

As we pressed as far forward as we possibly could, we found ourselves next to two young ladies who were standing on plastic crates. This gave them a boost of twelve inches or so.

"These crates were a great idea," said the blonde one, cracking her gum. "We really didn't need to buy them, you know. We could have ripped them off outside a convenient store."

The other girl, a clear-eyed redhead with natural ringlets, stole a glance at me. Clearly, she thought her friend was trying to shock this "elderly person" who was crowding in on their space.

The girls continued to congratulate themselves for their ingenuity and began swaying a bit from atop their crates. Suddenly, a slight crash froze the immediate crowd. In front of the Crate Twins an African-American couple had been sitting on tottery folding chairs. The motion of the crowd had toppled the well-dressed gentleman from his chair, and it now lay in pieces beside him. He struggled up, clasping his videocam as if it were the Hope diamond. His wife, still settled on her folding chair, gently brushed dust from his camel's-hair overcoat. Righting his snappy fedora, he tried to gain his composure, pushing aside the fragments of the ill-fated chair.

He smiled up at the Crate Twins. "Stupid of me to bring these chairs, anyway. My wife, though, she needs to sit." He gave her shoulder a loving pat. "Glad hers didn't go down."

The twins seemed semi-abashed but did not offer to get down from their crates.

"You girls really are blocking others' view," said a tiny lady in a gentle voice.

"Yeah, who do you think you are, the Statue of Liberty?" A teasing voice, not altogether gentle. Mine.

"People just don't have to stand behind us," the redhead remarked, miffed. "Anybody could have brought something to stand on. I'll have to write about this in my journal."

"Me, too," I muttered.

To our right, a group of Thirty-somethings were discussing the hazards of high cholesterol and the need for exercise. It almost seemed as if they were mounting a personal mission directed at a couple nearby who were noticeably overweight. Then someone lit a cigarette. The Thirties swooped down in a frenzy, lecturing and lambasting as

Tapestry

the man grabbed a couple of quick puffs before stomping out his Marlboro.

Generally, though, the conversation was amicable. Gathered for what was billed as a Great American Reunion, people swapped stories, discovered mutual interests, even mutual acquaintances. I heard one of the male Thirty-somethings mention he was an alum of a small college in Kentucky. Not only had he heard of my small Indiana alma mater, which plays in the same athletic conference, he had once attended a basketball camp there directed by a classmate of mine.

The recorded music now was giving way to the Marine Band and singing groups. This didn't seem to matter to the Thirties; they kept right on dispensing their learned diatribe. Louder, now . . . they seemed emboldened by their victory over the smoker.

"Oh, we hear the music—in the background," one man said. He was wearing a Harvard sweatshirt and a Boston Red Sox cap. I knew some of us would like to hear the music. Are we this conditioned to elevator music? Don't live performers rate respect, especially in front of the U.S. Capitol? "Well, how about turning down your volume?" I asked. I did the gentle, hand-on-the-arm assertiveness business—and smiled. It worked. In a few minutes the Thirties were speaking in hushed tones.

The familiar Ringwald arrangement of "The Battle Hymn of the Republic" followed the entrance of President and Mrs. Bush. I found myself singing along, softly, to this stirring anthem I'd so often sung in choirs. In my left ear came a beautiful tenor, the gentleman from Louisville whose chair had crashed. We exchanged smiles as we sang and tucked away a special little memory each of us had shared with a stranger.

An oversized TV screen to our right was visible to only those over six feet tall. A handsome young man wearing a yamulke gave a running narration of the onscreen activity. As he announced the entrance of the

Clintons and the Gores, pressing questions arose from onlookers such as, "What color is Hillary's hat?" "Do Bill and Al have on matching suits?" "Did they do anything with Chelsea's hair?"

I asked the young man if he'd been a worker for Clinton. He seemed so passionately turned on to the events of the day. He said he lives in Virginia, works in D.C. This was the first campaign he'd been active in, but he vowed it would not be the last. "We'll be back here in four years," he said. "After that, it'll be Al--"

We were then led in prayer by the gentle phrases of Dr. Billy Graham. The young Jewish man muttered softly and stared straight ahead. I remembered those Jewish students I taught in a New York school when school prayer was required. Refusing to bow their heads to pray to a Christian God, they always looked up at the ceiling and pretended to count the dots in the tiles. I thought of Psalm 121: "I will lift up my eyes to the hills from whence cometh my help." Instead of bowing my head, I raised my eyes to the brilliant blue sky, to the majesty of the Capitol dome. I could feel the young man near me doing the same. Later, however, during the playing of Aaron Copland's *Fanfare for the Common Man*, I noticed him crouched over in a near-fetal position behind the tiny lady who had first criticized the Crate Twins. There was no designated time on the program for him to pray.

When the actual words of the Inaugural Oath resounded through the excellent sound system, a shiver seemed to run through the crowd. In what other nation is power transferred so smoothly? Repeating the same words as every president since Washington, William Jefferson Clinton (known already to the nation as "just plain Bill") accepted the awesome mantle of authority and its responsibilities.

Another prayer from Dr. Graham, then the stunning poem from Maya Angelou, "In the Pulse of the Morning." Many people remained with heads bowed, thinking it was a prayer also. Her words seemed to speak truths to everyone, people of all races and creeds, even people who don't think they like poetry. Her eloquence bespoke her personal history and that of her people.

Following the new President's inaugural address, Senator Ford of Kentucky, the Master of Ceremonies, announced "The Star Spangled Banner" would be sung by Metropolitan Opera's Marilyn Horne. Again, necks craned to see the TV screen, to watch the performance. Surely, the audience would be expected to join in. I can't remember when I ever felt like singing the National Anthem as much as I did that day.

At first, no one sang. Feeling I'd tilted enough windmills for the day, I kept quiet. Then I heard a clear, strong soprano from nearby; others joined in a cameo moment frozen in memory. At the last note, puffs of smoke from a twenty-one gun salute dotted the sky as the Marine Band struck up "Hail to the Chief" for the first time for President Bill Clinton. I couldn't see his face, but I'm sure his eyes misted over as I've seen them do on TV. One thing about this new president—he's human.

We nodded our goodbyes to our fellow standees with whom we'd shared this glorious January morning. The Twins were packing their crates with their cameras and thermoses. "Hey, there, Miss Liberty," I said to the red-haired one. "Thanks for getting us started singing the National Anthem. You have a marvelous voice."

"Thanks," she said, reaching out for my hand. "I hope you put that in your journal, too." I don't know which was more brilliant, her smile or the sunlight on that glorious red hair.

TRAVELS WITH ROCI

Our first glimpse of Rocinante III occurred as we were leaving the Cleveland RV Show one blustery February night. Our hopes were as chilled as the wind off Lake Erie. After two hours of looking at motor homes, we found everything too luxurious—we were REAL campers, you know—and incompatible with our budget.

Suddenly, sandwiched between two 32-foot behemoths stood the answer to our demands. Called a Mini-Cruiser, it was small enough to be economical for vacationing and also to serve as a second car. Yet, it had the same conveniences John Steinbeck had specified in *Travels with Charley*—double bed, stove, furnace, refrigerator, lights, toilet, and storage space. (Note: Rocinante was the name of Don Quixote's horse. Steinbeck named his truck-camper Rocinante also).

Within a week, this compact little miracle stood in our driveway. Not content to wait for spring before we ventured forth with our new companion, as soon as the current Cleveland blizzard subsided, we struck out to our daughter's in the next state.

There we discovered a use for Roci that we hadn't anticipated. We spent our first night in our "turtle-shell," again borrowing Steinbeck's phrase, "camped" in daughter Pam's driveway in southern Indiana. When we awoke, a 6-inch snowfall had blessed us during the night. Inside, we were snug and well-rested; our little furnace whirred away as reliably as the one in our home. Since then, Roci frequently doubles as an extra bedroom when we visit any of our several married children. We feel we are less of a disruption in their homes or apartments. At home, we always have one more extra bedroom at our own house at holiday times; two or even three visitors can always bunk in Roci.

As a second car for us, Roci showed another dimension of versatility. There seemed to be no limit to the amount of groceries or flea market finds that could be stowed in Roci's hold. Picking up tennis partners and their gear was a snap in "The Motemobile" as friends liked to call it. Finding Roci is no problem in even the most crowded shopping center parking lot.

Once I became accustomed to driving a stick shift, I batted around town with ease. Only one incident clouds my memory. My husband and I were to meet for dinner at a favorite Italian restaurant. Unfortunately for Roci and me, it has a canopy. (You can guess what's coming.) The favorite Italian restaurant now has a new canopy, Roci is missing a rooftop luggage rack, and my insurance rate is a bit higher. I must constantly remind myself which car I'm driving.

Our photo albums bulge with memories of our Travels with Roci throughout the adjacent 48 states. Without a moment's hesitation—though using every iota of power those four cylinders could generate—Roci carried us over the Rockies and through Canada's Fraser River valley. We have parked for overnights along winding Colorado roads we could never have explored with a larger rig. We'd fall asleep listening to a rushing mountain stream outside our door and awaken to the awesome majesty of snow-capped mountains all around us. After a leisurely breakfast and perhaps a few casts for trout, we'd be on our way. Closer home, Roci offered tailgate partying at OSU football games or weekend jaunts to Amish country where apple-cheeked girls visited our campsite each morning selling delectable baked goods.

As you can determine, Roci is self-contained. It uses electric or propane. A battery in the rear can be switched on, and furnace, toilet, and lights run off this 12-volt battery that re-charges while traveling the next day. This feature enabled us to join the ranks of "primitive" campers and seek more scenic, secluded sites in woods, near water, or on hilltops where larger motorized camping rigs could never function untethered. Whenever possible, we would forego Interstates and instead travel the secondary roads that led to dozens of memorable places and people.

Roci has a full-width window across the rear of the cab. It's a perfect spot for passengers to view the countryside while traveling. I can close my eyes and bring up visions of the Rockies, Washington DC lighted at night, the Golden Gate Bridge, my first glimpse of Mt. Rushmore…all the while Woody Guthrie would be singing in my head, "This Land is Your Land."

After about a dozen years, as we looked toward retirement, more space and comfort for our travels seemed desirable. Again, we visited the RV Show, this time looking for a larger rig that we could tow and unhook if we chose. We still wanted that ability to drive to out-of-the-way spots without dragging our house behind us. Eventually, we found a rig that suited our needs and served us for many summers and vacation trips. In spite of the comfort of that 35-foot Holiday Rambler, re-living those Travels with Roci through photos and vivid memories never ceases to give us pleasure.

ONE SEPTEMBER MORNING

S tanding back, I admired the well-organized, expertly packed trunk of my car. Newton, my dear late husband, could not have done a better job, I told myself. Besides, it's only 7 a.m. and I'll soon be on my way to the Poconos. When did I ever get him on the road this early?

I was trying to be mentally flip, but, in reality, this getting "on the road again" without him was wrenching my heartstrings. Only six months before, his life had been snuffed out suddenly by a wayward blood clot. This would be my first venture into unknown territory without him. For twenty-plus years, we had spent summers and school vacations criss-crossing the country, towing our 35-foot travel trailer we called Walden. We really did live simply—though by twentieth-century standards, not Thoreau's.

After a walk-through of the house to make sure everything was secure, I did a last-minute check of my route. With my correctly folded map and cell phone within reach, I headed east on the Ohio Turnpike. Popping in a new CD saved especially for this trip, I relaxed and let Beethoven's moving Symphony No. 3, *Eroica,* fill my senses.

The sky was clear, and I could count on the sunrise to flood my windshield in another half-hour. It appeared this would be what my grown-up children call "a New York day." They remember their childhoods spent in upstate New York where summer skies often are breathtakingly blue and cloudless and temperatures blessedly in the 70s. Or would this be what I think of as a "Pippa Passes" day? A day that promises in Browning's words, "God's in his heaven, all's right with the world." So it seemed as the incomparable sounds of the Cleveland Orchestra buoyed my spirits, and the Ohio landscape flashed past.

Heading to a week-long writer's workshop in an unknown area seemed an ideal way to begin my newly assigned life as a single, just-turned-70 woman. I could have flown to Scranton, then taken transportation provided to the workshop site. But driving better suited my mood, and airline travel to smaller cities often requires hopscotching around the country. The monotony of turnpike travel gave me a chance to dwell on the dilemmas I'd encountered in the novel I was writing. Feedback from the other eleven writers in this workshop would help me unravel those, I hoped. Meanwhile, as they are wont to do at any time of day or night, my characters leaped upon my mind-stage for the next fifty miles or so.

As the orchestra mounted a staccato of brass and tympani, I realized the CD was ending. *Eroica* always leaves me breathless; it seems to define heroism, no matter how often I hear it. I drove on in the stillness, the final strains resounding in my consciousness.

Thinking perhaps I should check in with the rest of the world, I switched to the radio and tried to find a local station. By this time I had crossed into Pennsylvania. An announcer's raspy voice pierced the silence of my car. Thinking it was a commercial, I tried another station only to hear yet another overwrought voice. The words "This is real…" "A second plane has hit…" "New York's Twin Towers…" "It's a grisly war scene…" "people fleeing in terror…"

I drove on, not believing or even comprehending what I was hearing. Soon I realized that my arms seemed nearly paralyzed from gripping the steering wheel. White-knuckled, I kept driving, trying to make sense out of the staccato-like phrases bouncing from the radio. This was no War-of the-Worlds stunt. Terrorists had actually defiled our largest city and flown planes into the heart of Manhattan's financial district! At this moment, New Yorkers who had just reached their offices were trapped in burning, crumbling buildings or jumping in hopes of saving their lives.

At first, nothing but stubborn denial filled my mind: This is the never-invaded USA. How could such a debacle occur? How could these planes not have been detected? Hearing the word "hijackers" over and over, I realized that these appeared to be commercial airliners—our own—that had been taken over by evildoers.

Reality was creeping into my consciousness, blotting out my disbelief. Only one other time in my life had such helpless, bone-chilling fear gripped me. I'd been alone that time, too—a terrified ten-year-old, sitting in a Sunday afternoon movie, hearing about an attack on Pearl Harbor. I remember I'd hugged the trunk of a huge tree as I ran home, feeling for something safe and permanent.

Six decades later, I clutched my steering wheel as if my car enclosed me in a hurling capsule of safety. Fear and disbelief were giving way now to anger. I could feel a red rage behind my eyes and bile rising in my throat. I kept heading east, not even thinking about where I was going. I punched off the torrent of horrific details coming from my radio and silently prayed for those poor souls in the Twin Towers and their families. It seemed a feeble offering, at best.

A sign for Mo's Diner in the next town caught my eye. On Interstate 80, towns were few and far between. My stomach was rumbling, but food was the last thing on my mind. Yet, the idea of the warmth of human company drew me to the exit ramp.

Inside Mo's Diner, a group of local men—probably retirees who'd gathered for a regular weekly coffeeklatch—sat transfixed and mute before an overhead television. The only other Mo's customers were a young couple whose baby slept blissfully in one of those car seats that appear to be designed for space travel and a prim-looking sixty-ish woman who was helping her prim looking eighty-ish companion to the ladies' room. The lone server's nametag proclaimed brightly,

"Hi! I'm Millie." Treading heavily to and from the kitchen, she silently dispensed scrambled eggs, hotcakes, and poured coffee. Her heavily rouged cheeks contrasted with the naked fear in her eyes. When she poured my water, her hand shook slightly.

While I waited for an English muffin and coffee, I strained to hear the television although I didn't want to move closer to the Good Old Boys' Club. Tossing agitated shouts at one another now, they scraped their chairs as they pulled closer to the television. On the screen I could make out the image of a sprawling, smoking building and on the split screen that of a smoke-shrouded green field. Other places besides the New York buildings had evidently been hit. The knot in my stomach tightened and a cold finger of fear stabbed at my spine.

The couple with the baby, on their way to the cash register, stopped at my table. The Pentagon, they said, had been hit by a plane and also another plane had crashed in Somerset County, Pennsylvania. "About 80 miles from here," they filled me in. "South of Pittsburgh."

"My sister works in Manhattan," the young mother said. Her lips didn't seem to want to form the words.

The English muffin tasted like cardboard, but the coffee was rich and flavorful. After I'd asked Millie for a second cup, I dialed my cell phone for the conference where I was headed. "This call cannot be completed at this time," came the canned response. My placemat map of Pennsylvania told me I was about as far northeast of Pittsburgh as the site of that plane crash was southeast of that city. A vise-like feeling gripped me—a need to be with the people I love, in the place where I belong. Surely there would be no writers' conference.

Heading back west, the bleakness of the Interstate depressed me. Every car that passed seemed to have but a lone occupant; each face wore the same tense, drained expression that I felt on my own. A familiar route sign, U.S. 322, pointed northwest, a route that I knew would eventually take me to Cleveland's east side. Passing through the chain of small towns definitely slowed my progress, but seeing other people, going about their daily lives, gave me some sense that life would go on as usual.

By now it was around one o'clock in the afternoon. Hastily lettered signs were springing up on church lawns, *Come in and pray. God Bless America.* These were repeated in town after town. Flags fluttered all along the main streets. These sights buoyed my spirit and kept me alert—and kept me praying as well.

When I reached home, several hours passed before I could pry myself away from the television. All the horror I had heard on the car radio was now played out in my family room. As relieved as I was to be within the safety of my own four walls, the horror and anguish I saw on the faces flashing across the screen brought tears of empathy, a cold, gnawing fear, a wave of helplessness.

The phone's shrill demand pierced the droning television, forcing me to stifle my tears. The local hospital where I volunteer each week had put out a call for blood donors. The response was overwhelming. Could I come and help register donors? Of course. Here was a chance to do some small thing—anything—when I'd seen so many doing so much—firefighters, police officers, ordinary citizens acting with compassion toward others.

When I reached the hospital, though it was hundreds of miles away from the scenes of the infamous attacks, citizens of my home town had queued up and down several hallways to give blood for their fellow Americans. An anxious young mother with a fretful baby in a stroller...a bentover man pushing his wife in a wheelchair...a pair of teens, fear etched on their faces, holding tightly to each other's hands...a bank president whom I recognized, staring blankly at his *Wall Street Journal.* These and countless others had stood up from their supper tables and come to offer their lifeblood to victims of this unspeakable act.

Before the evening was over, we had reached capacity of blood that could be collected that day; we had to ask donors to return another day. There was no grumbling about waiting, then being turned away.

Once again, those prophetic lines of William Faulkner's that I cling to rang true for me. "I believe that man will not merely endure; he will prevail. I decline to accept the end of man."

PART FOUR
PERSONS I WISH I'D MET

Sen. Joseph E. McDonald

Capt. Edward J. Kennedy

News analyst: Dorothy Fuldheim

"EVERYONE OUGHT TO HAVE BEEN BORN POOR."
DOROTHY FULDHEIM

Milwaukee 1903

Anyone watching the stocky girl with flaming red hair who darted in and out of 6th Street storefront doorways in a Milwaukee slum might have thought she was a runaway. One minute she'd stop at a drug store, as if the grimy window's papier-mâché fisherman advertising cod-liver oil enthralled her. Next she'd zigzag along the teeming, littered street, dodging fruit vendors with sagging shoulders and rowdy afternoon newsboys, all the while stealing backward glances as if fearing attack dogs in pursuit.

Her jaw was clenched and her blue eyes steely with resolve. Not more than ten, she wore a faded, school-rumpled cotton dress, barely covering her knees, black stockings and scuffed, high-topped shoes. Clutching her school satchel to her chest, she walked faster now, as if her goal was in sight. With a bird-like glance in either direction, she bolted into a narrow alley where a few drab clapboard houses huddled together like beggars in the shadows of dingy stone tenements. A stifling stench rose from piles of garbage that offered themselves to hordes of green flies, while a mangy, one-eared dog slobbered over a splintered bone. The girl sidestepped a pile of horse droppings and lifted a rusted latch. A creaking gate swung open in a sagging fence that boasted startling mounds of blue morning glories, now closing their daily show. One more time, she thought, I've done it. I got home from school without anyone seeing this awful, ugly street where I live.

Inside the gate Dorothy Violet Schnell arrived in her own secluded world: a minuscule plot of stubby grass, a rope swing tied to a struggling weeping willow, a bench made of a discarded shutter and a few bricks. Here she entered her private retreat, her sanctuary from the filth and din of the streets around her. Off came the high-topped shoes and darned cotton stockings. Next, Dorothy pulled from her satchel the book she had borrowed yesterday from the next-door neighbor, Mrs. Dehni. She often ran errands for Mrs. Dehni and her many lady friends who came and went over there. In return, she was allowed to borrow books from the shelves at the top of the back stairs. Propping herself against the bench, she wriggled her bare toes in the grass and fondled the book before opening the cover of *Lady Randolph's Lover*.

Wafting over from next door, the sumptuous fragrance of Mrs. Dehni's solitary lilac bush wrapped Dorothy in a dream world. Nothing smelled as heavenly as lilacs, Dorothy thought. She often told her mother she would like to sleep on a bed of lilacs and have them strewn on her path wherever she'd go. Her mother, who believed her children were exceptional, always told her she could do anything she wished. So what was so impossible about sleeping in lilacs, already?

Soon Dorothy was reveling in her book, totally shutting out the thumps and whacks coming from the open cellar door of the Schnells' meager house. If she heard them at all. These were everyday sounds. Her brother David, four years younger and already home from school, was probably perched on an apple box, swatting away rats while their mother did the family's laundry. With a little luck Dorothy could read a chapter or two before her mother would emerge from the cave-like cellar. Squinting in the afternoon sunshine, she'd call Dorothy to help hang out the Schnell family's tired-looking, tattered laundry. The warm May breeze would dry it before supper time.

Dorothy turned the pages eagerly. Even a borrowed dime novel was a luxury. In the Schnell household there was scarcely money enough for rent, food, and scant clothing. Dorothy dreaded the trips she'd make to the butcher when he'd say, "Tell your mother I have to have something on the bill." Many times there was no meat in their house for days. Apples and potatoes were cheap, and Bertha Schnell made vast quantities of soup from each to help keep her family warm and their stomachs full.

Still, Dorothy's own life was not nourishment enough. She turned to books to feed the hungering of a young soul, yearning for romance and beauty, a respite from the poverty in which she lived. Herman Schnell, Dorothy's father, was a good man, but making a living for his family wasn't his long suit. He tried to sell insurance; he tried to sell clothes. He wasn't very good at either, but he had a great reverence for learning and for the beauty of language. One thing he and Bertha agreed upon was the importance of their children's education. Both parents had left their native lands while still in their teens, arrived penniless in America, and mastered a new language to enable them to survive in their new surroundings. Herman had come from Germany, Bertha Wishner from Russia. They had met and married near the east coast of their new country, but after the births of their two daughters, Dorothy and Janette, they had moved to Milwaukee. David was born soon after their arrival. Milwaukee had a large German immigrant population, and the Schnells had relatives there. Herman and Bertha had hopes for a brighter future in Milwaukee, but life had remained harsh for them.

With flimsy coats and holes in their mittens and their shoes, Dorothy, Janette, and their brother David trudged the two miles to school and back through torrential rains and blinding snowstorms. They never had three cents for a bowl of soup at school but ate an apple and stale gingerbread for lunch instead.

"A great wall separated the children who had three cents for soup and a nickel for ice cream and those who had no money for such luxuries," Dorothy was to write decades later in her book *I Laughed, I Cried, I Loved*. "No one who has not known poverty, lived in it, with it, and been ground down by it, can understand its terrifying effect." She never forgot the humiliation of poverty. In her mid-eighties she told Cleveland *Plain Dealer's* Mary Strassmeyer, "Everyone ought to have been born poor. You have more respect for people when you become successful." Twice a week, in spite of searing summer heat or the most bone-chilling winter day, Bertha Schnell allowed Dorothy to walk twelve blocks to the Milwaukee Public Library and twelve blocks back. Her only caution to her book-starved older daughter was that she wear a bonnet to protect her face and neck from the summer sun or mittens, ragged though they might be, to prevent frostbitten fingers in winter.

She needn't have warned Dorothy about this, for the girl was already careful about her fair skin. Secretly, she longed for a graceful white neck and fluttering hands like her Aunt Molly's. Dorothy adored her Aunt Molly, her mother's younger sister, who modeled dresses at a department store. Remarkably, by age twenty-five, Molly Davidson had buried three husbands and adopted their collective group of nine sons. When she came to visit Dorothy's mother, the Schnells' shabby house exhaled an aura of luxury for days afterward. Aunt Molly's perfume wafted through the boxlike rooms, punctuated by the lingering sound of her staccato-laden syllables. She enunciated her own unique brand of wisdom: "The morning sun is best for sleep. That's when your strength and health are fortified." She also said, "Tea is good for only one thing: to be a conveyor of jam. And it has to be peach jam. It kisses your cheeks and makes them glow."

Aunt Molly must surely have been the most beautiful woman in Milwaukee. She had an hourglass figure, and she moved sinuously, using her God-given grace to her best advantage. Few males did not fall victim to her coquetry and beauty. But she was not destined to be a married woman for much of her life. Her first two husbands fell to their deaths at their work, and the third died after a brief illness. Fortunately, there had been a total inheritance of $16,500 and a large house from Husband Number Two. The indefatigable Molly insisted she would keep all nine of her stepsons with her—to the consternation of her practical-minded sister Bertha. She warned Molly that boys would be hard to raise and that she was letting herself in for a fate worse than a job. Molly would toss her pretty head and sniff into her scented, lace-trimmed handkerchief. "So, what am I to do? Throw these boys out into the street? Of course, they will stay with me . . . they are mine, and God wants me to keep them." Dorothy would watch her aunt's luminous blue-violet eyes brim with tears as she gathered the boys, aged three to the thirteen-year-old twins, around her. Bertha Schnell would shake her head and pour her sister another cup of tea. There was never any use arguing with Molly when she related her conversations with God. After Aunt Molly's visits, Dorothy would peer at her own pre-pubescent image in the cracked mirror in the kitchen when no one else in the family was looking. Were her eyes as wide-set as Aunt Molly's? True, Dorothy had the thick auburn hair, but when she was allowed to wear it up, would hers look as gloriously elegant? Tying a tattered bedsheet around her waist, she would practice swishing when she walked, as Aunt Molly did. "Don't walk straight, swish a little," Aunt Molly had told her. "This makes a man feel you are not a waitress or a grocery store clerk but you are a woman whose business is to be a woman." Years later, Dorothy would tell her Aunt Molly's story in her book, *Three and a Half Husbands*. It was considered by a major producer as material for the musical theatre but, to Dorothy's disappointment, that never took place.

Dorothy longed for some perfume, for her aunt had told her that she put a different perfume on each of her petticoats, just as the Medici women did in the time of Leonardo da Vinci. But perfume was as out of reach for Dorothy as the diamond rings her aunt wore—one from each of her husbands. Once Dorothy's brother David came in and found her arrayed in her sheet and swishing across the rough, bare floors of their home. He ran back outside to get their sister Janette, and the two of them poked fun at Dorothy until she flung the sheet off and ran outside to the solace of her willow tree and her books.

If it was her day to go to the library, she could escape her brother and sister for hours. On a stifling summer day, Dorothy would hurry to catch up with Jack, who delivered ice to everyone in the neighborhood for their iceboxes. She'd politely beg slivers from his wagon. After carefully wiping the sawdust from the jagged pieces he'd hand her, Dorothy would savor their soothing coolness on her parched lips and picture herself sipping tall, frosty drinks on the deck of a luxurious ocean liner, her deck chair surrounded by a cluster of admiring swains. Near the reeking Milwaukee River, Dorothy would pass one of the city's largest breweries. The air around there hung in dense, malt-laden sheets, prickling Dorothy's nostrils unpleasantly. Workers huddled in groups over their dinner pails, and a lethargic game of horseshoes was in progress on a dusty strip of grass. A few workers waved, for Dorothy, with her armload of books, was a familiar passer-by. "There goes little Miss Library Lady," one grimy worker called out in a friendly tone.

These twice-weekly trips to the library were Dorothy's keys to locked doors of enchantment and wonder. By the time she was ten or eleven, she had unconsciously realized the mental limitations of Mrs. D's library of dime novels and yearned for more challenging reading. She discovered Shakespeare at an early age and read and re-read Dickens' works, easily putting herself into their settings of London's slums. The novels of Thackeray, Jane Austen, and Charlotte Brontë utterly consumed her romantic young soul.

Once she had selected her quota of books to borrow and had checked them out with the waspish librarian, who cluck-

clucked her approval or occasionally frowned an objection over her choices, Dorothy was ready for her special treat. No trip to the library was complete without "The Stairs." She stole out of the main reading room and waited, cat-like, until there were no people near the twin marble staircases on either side of the lobby. Creeping to the top of one of the stairways, her books cradled in one arm, Dorothy lifted the train of an imaginary green taffeta gown and began her promenade down to the street level. She could hear the train rustling luxuriously as she glided down, smiling and nodding graciously to the awed stares of friends and would-be suitors she pictured watching her. Reaching the bottom, she turned, a portrait of elegance and grace, dropped her train, and blew kisses to the crowd.

Whether she was an actress, a duchess, or an operatic soprano never cluttered Dorothy's mind. But always the dress was green taffeta with a train that rustled; always she reveled in the adoring attention of her admirers. Someday, she'd vow, I'll have all the taffeta dresses I want, and people will clap and cheer for me. So enfolded was Dorothy in her make-believe world, she never noticed the knot of library clerks bunched at the top of the stairs, watching her descend. Dorothy, with her stocky figure and her flowing red hair, had become an accustomed sight, but none of them would disturb her flight of fancy. Had she known they were watching, she would probably have waved to them and flung kisses.

Cleveland 1973

A strident see-sawing of strings, brook-like ripples of flutes and clarinets, and the oboe's authoritative note drifted up toward the frescoed ceiling. Members of the Cleveland Orchestra shifted in their chairs and arranged their music, readying themselves for the Thursday evening all-Strauss concert. A mushy, early-April snowfall, not unusual for Cleveland, had slowed concertgoers' arrivals, but Severance Hall was filling steadily now. Outer garments exhaled the pungent aroma of wet wool, a contrast to the baskets of fragrant flowers on the stage apron. The only sounds from the audience were discreet coughs and the rustle of programs as seasoned music lovers poured over their program notes.

When the clock's hands crept past eight, a barely perceptible stir rippled through the hall. Coughs were more frequent. Heads began turning. A low hum of voices rose as patrons reminded one another that the Cleveland Orchestra's Thursday night concerts dependably began on the hour. Ushers positioned themselves sedately along the aisles, their faces locked passively, as if hoping their presence evidenced a normal state of affairs. At 8:23 a whispered swell swept forward from the rear of the hall. Two ushers were escorting a bustling, diminutive, red-haired woman to the only two still-vacant orchestra seats. Following her was a younger female companion wearing oversized glasses and a halo of white-blond curls,. The redhead—gracious, chatting—smiled up at one usher, then at the other. Patrons seated near the aisle caught a drift of French perfume, a flash of a heavy jeweled bracelet, and shoes dyed to match the rustling, green taffeta dress. They also heard words of sincere regret for her late arrival, caused by a traffic tie-up.

With brief greetings to those seated nearby, the two women scarcely settled into their seats when the house lights dimmed. Maestro Lorin Maazel entered to sedate applause and took up his baton. The Cleveland Orchestra's evening with Strauss could now begin.

In the next to the last row, two out-of-town businessmen, who were passing the evening hours by taking in a weeknight concert, exchanged puzzled looks. One remarked to the other that he didn't realize Cleveland boasted royalty.

This story circulated with alacrity in Cleveland in the mid-1970's. Truth or legend, it symbolizes the homage and respect the city paid Dorothy Fuldheim, pioneer television commentator and analyst. She was an anchorwoman before the term was coined.

Far more than achieving vapid celebrity status, Dorothy Fuldheim attached herself to every Cleveland family. Though her fans might not always agree with her, they felt free to tell her so. ("Hey, Red, you were all wet last night," a truck driver once called out as he passed her at a downtown corner.) But a window washer delighted in telling her that his wife thought she should run for President. A friend to drivers of cabs as well as members of Congress, Dorothy Fuldheim daily affirmed the worth of every individual she met. "She was a queen, but she didn't act like one," one close associate is fond of saying. Shouts and greetings followed her wherever she went, and people frequently sidled up to her in crowds and asked if they could touch her. At an opening day for the Cleveland Indians, she attracted more attention than the city's civic leaders or the president of the American League. By 1973, Dorothy Fuldheim, at age eighty, was the longest running personality on television. She had traveled widely with her wealthy friend she identifies only as Roseka, and had gained respect on the lecture circuit. After she married Clevelander Milton Fuldheim, she came to Cleveland's flagship Scripps Howard station, WEWS-TV, in 1947 when she was fifty-four. Not just a news reader—a talking head—she was a news analyst and a commentator in the true sense of the word. With no model to follow, she had fashioned her television news broadcasts in a format which pleased her—and evidently pleased her superiors, her sponsors, and her viewers. She would continue to hold forth for nearly four decades. The late Donald Perris, then-general manager at WEWS-TV, confirms that she had offers from television stations in larger markets, but she chose to remain in Cleveland.

In 1984, she conducted her last interview, by satellite with then-President Ronald Reagan, only hours before she suffered the first of several strokes that would leave her helpless for the remaining five years of her life. Despite her powerful intellect and awe-inspiring storehouse of knowledge, her lightning-quick mind and years of globe-circling to interview the affluent, the powerful, and the infamous, Dorothy Fuldheim grappled throughout her life with fears borne of a childhood of grinding poverty. She endured devastating tragedies in her adult life, particularly the death of her beloved daughter, Dorothy Louise, at age sixty. In her commentaries emerged traces of a wistful searching for a truth and serenity not found in erudition and science. In some of her interviews, especially in the 1980s, a yearning surfaced for a dimension of happiness she saw in others' lives but never experienced in her own. Only those closest to Dorothy Schnell Fuldheim sensed this longing for something more in life. It was a carefully concealed facet of her nature. Generally, she lived and moved and worked in the aura of confidence and ebullience she had created for herself.

Yet, Sam Miller, the cherished friend who became her guardian in the final years of her life, had these words from Ecclesiastes inscribed on her tombstone in Cleveland's Park Synagogue Cemetery: *With much wisdom, there is much sorrow.* "She was the unhappiest woman I ever knew, a tragic figure," Miller says. But through the decades, to her friends and colleagues and to the world at large, the phenomenal, durable redhead was Ultimate Authority—Mother Confessor—Best Friend—A Window on the World.

Excerpted from *Dorothy Fuldheim: The First First Lady of Television News*©Patricia M. Mote 1997 Quixote Publications.

"STAND YOUR GROUND!"
JOSEPH E. MCDONALD

Dedicated to the memory of my father, who kept alive for our family the memory of his grandfather for whom he was named.

Pulling his pocket watch from his vest, Joseph tried to match hours to miles. He stretched his lanky, travel-weary body as best he could on the bone-hard train seat. Sleep was hopeless as the clanking Baltimore & Ohio lurched from side to side, lumbering through the leafless Maryland hills.

"You'll be glad for sure, Congressman McDonald, when we pull into Fred'rick station." The friendly-faced conductor grinned. "You kin stretch yore legs while the train takes on water. Only another hour now."

And soon, Joseph thought, I'll be back in Washington, taking my seat on January 2, 1850, as the Thirty-first Congress resumes.

A well-liked, thirty-year-old lawyer, Joseph McDonald's fellow Hoosiers in Indiana's Eighth District had sent him to the nation's Congress as its youngest lawmaker. Stepson of a diligent farmer and apprenticed to a saddlemaker at age fourteen, Joseph was respected for earning his education as well as his for his fairness and integrity.

Now, halfway through his two-year term, Joseph felt the yoke of responsibility bearing down. These were troubled times. Slender ties of compromise binding the peace between northern and southern states for nearly three decades were straining and weakening month by month. Northern abolitionists protested the extension of slavery to the new territories; southerners shouted for their rights, as citizens of sovereign states, to protect their plantation way of life that depended upon slavery.

Shifting his cramped position again, Joseph pulled a dog-eared journal from his valise. When he took the oath as a congressman last year, Joseph had copied Amendment X from the Bill of Rights as a guidepost for his own decision-making: *"The powers not delegated to the United States by the Constitution nor prohibited by it to the States, are reserved to the states respectively or to the people."*

He affirmed this states' rights principle of democracy that Thomas Jefferson had insisted should be part of the Constitution. Yet he did not believe in one person owning another. How could he in good conscience go along with states that supported slavery?

After Joseph's election to Congress had been confirmed, Zebulon Beard, the wise, respected attorney with whom he had read law, took Joseph aside. Drawing the eager new lawmaker up by both his coat lapels, Zebulon said, "Do not be untrue to yourself in deference to another or so diffident that you fail in your duty." Zebulon knew mild-mannered Joseph disliked friction with others. Frequently he would address his young student in a stern, abrupt voice, "Stand your ground!" Zebulon's advice had already shepherded Joseph through some courtroom battles when he rode the circuit, traveling from town to town, following the judge, trying cases.

Noticing the portly gentleman next to him had nudged his valise for the second time, Joseph stowed his journal and pushed the valise farther beneath the seat. Looking out over the barren fields, he recalled the week-long stagecoach journey over frozen, rutted Indiana roads to Cumberland, Maryland, where he had boarded the train for Washington. In his mind's eye, he caught a glimpse, like a gently tinted portrait, of his wife Nancy Ruth and their two small sons, Ezekiel and

Malcolm, standing at their front gate. Joseph knew tears glistened in Nancy Ruth's soft, brown eyes, but she had not let him see them. To keep his loved ones in sight, Joseph had leaned as far as he dared from the stage window until his family's tiny figures drifted into the pearl-gray morning mist.

Nancy Ruth, a doctor's daughter, loved politics. Washington's excitement would have pleased her, but the young couple had agreed that life there was too rough, too expensive. Joseph would return to his lodging at Hill's Boarding House as he had done during last year's session.

After a quick stroll around the dank, dismal Frederick station, Joseph re-entered the railway car and stopped short. A knot of people surrounded a familiar figure now seated at the end of the car. Henry Clay! The revered Kentuckian, at age seventy-three, was still a bulwark of the Senate. His efforts for the Missouri Compromise had saved the union thirty years before. Now he was called upon again although he was suffering from tuberculosis.

Joseph folded himself into his seat and strained to hear what was happening. Eager reporters hovered like starving birds around Senator Clay, hoping for a preview of what the nation could expect when the Senate resumed.

Clay drew himself up forcefully, his voice carrying throughout the car. "Gentlemen of the press, I appreciate your kind attention." Senator Clay treats everyone like the gentleman that he is, thought Joseph. He memorized the Senator's features—proud, high forehead; long, serious face; piercing, close-set eyes that seemed to look everywhere at once.

The orator's still-powerful voice continued. "I am pondering a comprehensive scheme that, in its finality, will offer a method of settling the whole question of slavery and the new territories and states. I have, as yet, not worked out all of the details of this scheme, but when I do, you, sirs, will most certainly be informed." He beamed assurance to his listeners and nodded their dismissal.

Politely murmuring their thanks, the reporters scurried off the train. They prized any quotable words from the man who had worked out the Missouri Compromise that had cemented the nation's fissures for nearly thirty years.

Joseph shivered. That compromise had been when he was not much older than Malcolm. Now, he, Joseph, is part of the same Congress with Henry Clay, the Great Compromiser, as well as with Senator Daniel Webster and Senator John C. Calhoun. Guiding lights in the Senate for the past forty years, though each of them represented a distinctly different section of the nation.

After a tiresome, body-bruising night, Joseph awoke to pale streaks of light glimmering around the panels covering the overhead openings of the railway car. A child whimpered near the front. Close by, a haggard gentleman's raspy cough woke several others.

"Washin'ton Station. Everybody off here." The conductor beamed proudly as if he owned the B & O. Joseph glimpsed a manservant collecting Senator Clay's luggage. He had heard Clay's servant was a freed black man. Gathering his own few belongings, Joseph stepped off the train and headed through the slushy streets towards Hill's Boarding House.

True to his promise, in a few weeks Clay presented a plan to the Senate to settle all questions, or so he declared, in the controversy between free and slave states, growing out of the subject of slavery. Throngs of hopeful listeners waited in a dawn-gray, chilling mist to pass into the galleries. Inside, Joseph and other congressmen found themselves pressed to the rear wall, elbowing one another for standing room. Mustiness of rain-damp, woolen garments prickled their nostrils. The drone of male voices rose as tension mounted.

"They say there's no orator in America his equal," Joseph said to a colleague. "Move in here, sir."

A short barrel-chested member from Pennsylvania nodded his thanks and squeezed in front of Joseph. From his six-foot advantage, Joseph had a clear view of the podium Clay would soon mount.

"Have you never heard him?" the Pennsylvanian asked. "He plays that voice of his like an organ."

Holding the session of the Senate and the visitors as if in a trance, Clay spoke clearly of what he deemed necessary for a sound compromise, one that should demand no sacrifice of great principle by either side; yet, it should require concessions of opinion and interest by each side.

"Such a well-thought-out plan," Joseph leaned down to speak into the Pennsylvanian's ear.

"He speaks with tremendous authority. His mind is like a well-tuned machine," his comrade whispered.

But as the elder statesman outlined his resolutions, one by one, many faces in the chamber took on puzzled expressions.

"He's all but excludin' slavery from the territories, ain' he?" asked a rangy Tenneseean standing next to Joseph. There was a trace of alarm in his soft voice. "Lettin' the new states decide."

"But he's for toughening the Fugitive Slave Law," Joseph answered in his comrade's ear. The abolitionists of the North would not favor that part of Clay's plan, but Joseph knew Southerners would praise it.

How would the people of his Hoosier state feel about it, Joseph wondered. Many were descended from Kentucky families, and southern sympathies ran high in Indiana. Joseph felt his heart pounding under his stiff white shirt.

In the weeks that followed, voices swelled in protest. The Great Compromiser's resolutions would not sail through the Congress without heated debate. Presenting arguments for the southern states four weeks later was John C. Calhoun of South Carolina. But Calhoun was too ill to deliver his speech of objection himself.

Joseph felt twinges of compassion as the pain-wracked Calhoun hobbled into the chamber on the arm of another senator and handed his speech to Senator Mason of Virginia to read. Between fits of coughing, Calhoun settled himself in his chair and wrapped his black cloak around him. The familiar mane of iron-gray hair framed his wasted features and sunken eyes, making him look like a dying man.

Senator Mason began in a soft monotone: "The time for compromise is past..." Calhoun's gloomy words repeated the argument he'd hammered out many times before: The Federal government is ruled by a northern majority unfriendly to the southern states. "We have borne the wrongs and insults of the North long enough."

"He didn't really offer a plan," Joseph said to his colleagues at the boarding house that evening. "All he did was raise objections to Clay's resolutions."

"It would seem he's drivin' a deeper wedge than ever," said a red-faced Free Soiler from Ohio. The solemn congressmen passed steaming platters and bowls and ate in troubled silence.

In his tiny, box-like room that night, Joseph still volleyed with himself as to how he would vote on the issue of fugitive slaves. Senator Clay upheld this razor-sharp resolution certain to pacify the southern states and keep the union together. Yet, could he, Joseph, possibly vote for a measure based upon one man or woman or child as another's property, to be returned like a runaway cow or horse? He searched his conscience and prayed longer than usual for guidance.

Throughout the month after Calhoun's speech, anticipation mounted for the plan of the third member of what Washington called the Triumvirate—Daniel Webster, Senator from Massachusetts. As when Clay spoke, visitors and Congressmen streamed to the Capitol, filed into the galleries and waited restlessly for several hours to hear the "Godlike Daniel" address the Senate. The crowd was reported by a Washington paper to be larger than any previous occasion.

Heat from bodies packed tightly together hung like invisible sheets in the chamber. Water was served at specified intervals. Ladies were permitted to sit on the first floor where the scent of lavender water mingled with the headiness of the tobacco aroma clinging to the lawmakers' clothing.

"He'll be coming in soon," Joseph said to his colleagues. "He never keeps crowds waiting. I've heard." Joseph and some of his House colleagues had shrewdly fashioned makeshift seats from stacks of documents they'd found at the rear of the chamber.

"He's worth waiting for," a Massachusetts lawmaker said, his chest puffed out with pride. Webster was a legend in his state.

Daniel Webster, in his familiar oratorical garb—blue waistcoat with brass buttons and tails and buff-colored breeches—mounted the podium. At first, he spoke slowly, seeming to labor at what he was saying.

"Mr. President, I wish to speak today, not as a Massachusetts man, nor as a northern man, but as an American, and a member of the Senate of the United States...I speak today for the preservation of the Union. Hear me for my cause." Senator Webster's dark eyes blazed, but his voice dragged strangely with meaningless pauses.

He declared that secession of the southern states was an impossibility. "Nothing can break the Mississippi Valley in two."

"Not so," a faltering voice rasped from the chamber floor. "The Union can be broken!" The ailing Calhoun shook his fist, then sank back in his chair among his robes.

Senator Webster caught his stride and persisted for more than three hours. The thrust of his massive head and powerful shoulders dared his listeners to disagree with him. Congressmen and spectators, statue-like, riveted their eyes upon him.

"Listen to the way he reasons," Joseph whispered to his Ohio colleague. "Every thought becomes a link in an iron chain of reason."

To the amazement of the packed house, Webster upheld the Fugitive Slave Law. He declared any officer who took an oath to uphold the Constitution was bound by law to return runaway slaves. Slaves were personal property.

Joseph and many others stared in disbelief at Senator Webster. How dared this great statesman turn his back on his party's views and the strong belief of his own section of the country? In his mind's eye, Joseph saw a black man led, like a runaway animal, back to a southern plantation.

Is this what moral courage is? Joseph asked himself. Is a lawmaker supposed to vote his own conscience and forget his duty to the people who elected him? How he wished he could talk with Zebulon Beard. He could hear Zeb's throaty voice with its Hoosier twang: "...do not be so diffident that you fail in your duty."

Joseph knew the time for his duty was coming. The voting would soon begin on the compromise resolutions. Many members of the House railed against Webster's position. Some were northern Whigs, some were Free Soilers. Even New England had turned its back on its noble Daniel Webster.

"Yet," Joseph said at dinner one night, "Senator Webster said he didn't speak as a Massachusetts man or as a northerner, but as an American. Isn't that what we all are? What's Indiana without the Union? Or Tennessee? Or California, for that matter?" He looked around the table at his comrades' stunned faces for a flicker of reassurance.

But no one spoke. In the cabbage rose-papered dining room at Hill's Boarding House, the silence was deafening. Only the clink of china and silver eased the tension as the men kept on eating, eyes fixed on their plates.

Setting his jaw, Joseph laid his fork down carefully, gently pushed back his chair, and walked out onto the porch into the just-spring twilight. Though his heart felt gripped in a vise, Joseph could hear Zebulon Beard's stern words throbbing in his brain: "Stand your ground!"

During the months to follow Joseph would stand firm many times upon what he now knew he firmly believed. Following Webster's example, sacrificing whatever his own political future might be, Joseph would uphold all measures of compromise offered to save the Union.

As both houses of Congress debated the resolutions, the pall of death shrouded Washington. A few weeks after Webster's speech, the ailing Senator Calhoun died. Then in July came President Zachary Taylor's death after a brief illness contracted following Fourth of July festivity. Flags drooped at half-mast in Washington's summer heat. Congress again halted as the nation grieved for its leader.

Joseph scanned the hushed crowd of mourners filing through the Capitol rotunda to pay their respects to the dead President. The bold colors of the Stars and Stripes, folded across the President's coffin, piqued Joseph's conscience, reminding him of his business at the Capitol—helping to preserve the Union that flag stands for. "Sometimes I feel like I'm watching actors on a stage," he mused, "like all this isn't really happening to me,"

In the dog-days of summer, events in the Congress at last quickened. The new president, Millard Fillmore, believed in Clay's compromise measures, and passage neared reality. A mood of cautious optimism blanketed the Congress. "Home by harvest" became a daily slogan for

Joseph and his midwestern colleagues. Surely, they thought, the session would adjourn in a few weeks. He ached to cast his final votes and be a part of the passage of the resolutions. At least, he hoped with all his heart they would pass and stave off the secession of the southern states.

By the time President Fillmore signed the Compromise of 1850 into law in September, Joseph had, indeed, voted his conscience. He supported with fervor and conviction every measure of the Compromise. Along the way, he had to learn to ignore the disapproval of some of his fellow congressmen. And he knew there were voters back home whom he would disappoint.

Now heading back to Indiana, gauze-like images of cornfields, sycamore trees, and his family's faces sharpened each hour that the train labored west. His heart was thudding as hard as when the train took him to Washington for the first time. Even thinking of the tiresome stage ride ahead failed to dampen his soaring spirits. He prayed for fine weather to make the journey easier. Autumn rains could slow the journey to only a mile or two an hour. Bridges would wash away, making fording swollen streams necessary.

In a corner of his mind, Joseph harbored a thought that he should not run for re-election. Perhaps he should practice law and possibly serve his own state in some way before trying to return to Washington. "I have so much to learn," he thought. "When I'm more seasoned and our sons are older might be time enough to try for Washington again…maybe as a Senator…to sit in that chamber where Clay and Webster served." Joseph's scalp prickled at the thought.

Bracing his leg against the empty seat in front of him, he penned a final statement about the Thirty-first Congress in his creased, soot-stained journal. "Even though I was more a 'looker' than an 'actor,' I voted what I believed, and I watched and listened and learned from some of the most courageous men this nation has ever known. I learned what it means to 'Stand your ground.'"

Note: Joseph McDonald did not run for re-election to the House of Representatives. Instead, he became Indiana's first elected Attorney General, a post he held for two terms. He then entered into law practice in Indianapolis. In 1871, he was elected to the United States Senate.

The author gratefully acknowledges the debt owed to the McDonald family history and also for the use of Senator Joseph E. McDonald's personal papers, housed in the Lilly Library at Indiana University, Bloomington.

Additional sources:

Commager, Henry Steele. *Documents of American History.* 10th Ed. Englewood Cliffs NJ: Prentice Hall 1988.

Kennedy, John F. *Profiles in Courage.* New York: Harper & Row. 1955.

CAPTAIN EDWARD J. KENNEDY: A WORTHY SMALLTOWN CITIZEN

If there had been a citizen of the year award in Berea, Ohio, around the beginning of the twentieth century, surely Edward J. Kennedy's name would have been engraved upon it. At his passing in 1924 at age 82, his hometown newspaper, the *Enterprise*, stated "(his career) has been more eventful and outstanding than that of any other individual in the history of the village." It went on to say, "…it is doubtful if there is any individual in the community who has done more to promote the welfare and prosperity of Berea than Captain Kennedy."

His life as soldier, prisoner of war, survivor of America's worst peacetime maritime disaster, entrepreneur, and political leader exemplifies that of a true national hero.

Edward Kennedy was not a native Berean or even an Ohioan. His family didn't live in one of the proud Victorian homes on what was known as "God's side of town." In fact, he didn't even have a family that can easily be traced. By the time he was twelve, he was an orphan and, perhaps following Horace Greeley's advice to "Go West, young man," he left New York and went to Ypsilanti, Michigan.

Presumably, he lived with relatives or interested people who encouraged him to finish high school in Michigan. Then he went to Berea to work for John Baldwin, the founder of Baldwin University. A relative or Methodist church perhaps sponsored him as a student and helped him get work with Mr. Baldwin.

He had not yet completed his first year at Baldwin University when Ft. Sumter was fired upon in 1861. At nineteen, Edward Kennedy was among the first to enlist in the 7th Ohio Volunteer Infantry for three months. Then he reenlisted for three years. At the Battle of Cross Lanes, West Virginia, he was wounded and taken prisoner. He was exchanged and rejoined his regiment. Wounded at the Battle of Spring Hill in Tennessee, Kennedy was again taken prisoner. Altogether he was confined for a total of fourteen months in the prisons of Libby, Salisbury, and the horrific Andersonville.

Writing a column years later for the Berea *Advertiser's* "Camp Fire Chat," Kennedy described the inhumane conditions at Andersonville. "The owner of Hades himself could not have selected a more eligible location of his hellish work than this dreary, barren plain, encircled by a dense forest, almost untouched by the hand of man." He told how the prisoners were permitted to make only a crude shelter of two upright pieces of wood over which they stretched anything they could get in the shape of cloth. "Not everyone had this shelter, as the rags used to make the tent were needed by many to cover their nakedness… When on every side of Andersonville is an almost impenetrable forest of timber and yet we were denied the privilege of cutting it and making for ourselves huts and houses to keep out the heat of summer and the cold of winter."

He asked, "Can any nation or people excuse or apologize for this wrong? At one time within this prison pen of 13 to 15 acres were confined 35,000 prisoners." The graveyard outside with its 15,000 little white stones marks the places of the dead and tells the cruelties that took place there although the stockade has long ago been removed. At the close of the war, the prison superintendent, Captain Wirz, was convicted of murder and hanged.

In April 1865, shortly after the close of the Civil War, the river steamer *Sultana* pulled out of the New Orleans harbor. Built in Cincinnati, the *Sultana's* voyage began innocently enough. A sidewheeler, she held only about 100 paying passengers, a cargo of sugar, and nearly 100 livestock. By the time the steamer departed Vicksburg, where repairs were hastily made to a leaking boiler, the *Sultana* had taken on more than 2,000 veterans, mostly Union prisoners of war returning home. Some 2,300 people packed aboard the steamer. Incredibly, its legal limit was 376 passengers.

Edward Kennedy was among these veterans, released after months of imprisonment at Andersonville, "the hell of Georgia." He could hardly believe he was on his way home. He wrote of his first night at Andersonville, looking up into the bright sky and seeing the Big Dipper, the same Dipper whose stars he'd counted so often. He wondered if he'd ever see that Dipper and count its stars again in his Ohio home.

The boat labored up river against a strong current with its overload of ragged, weak and emaciated former prisoners. A leaky boiler caused a stop in Memphis for another hasty repair. One of the officers reportedly said, "I'd give all the interest I have in this steamer if we were safely landed at Cairo, Illinois." There the veterans were to be put on trains and taken to their home states. They eagerly looked forward to seeing the shoreline of Illinois, the first Union state they would see.

But ten miles up river from Memphis, the *Sultana* exploded into a massive fireball visible several miles away. Riverboats rushed to rescue victims, but it was too late for most. The explosion killed many almost instantly. Others met their fate in the muddy, frigid Mississippi. Most of the soldiers were so weakened from battle and the rigors of prison camps that they had little energy to stay afloat. Two out of every three of the passengers were killed outright or drowned in the cold waters of the Mississippi.

One survivor said, "When I got about 300 yards away from the boat, clinging to a heavy plank, the whole heavens seemed to be lighted up by the conflagration. Hundreds of my comrades were fastened down by the timbers of the decks and had to burn while the water seemed to be one solid mass of human beings struggling with the waves." This is an anonymous quote, but it must have been the disastrous scene that confronted Edward Kennedy as he clung with his burned limbs to a piece of wreckage for five hours. Rescuers hauled his half-dead form to Adams Hospital in Memphis. He spent months recovering and had to use crutches for some time.

The story of the *Sultana*, labeled the worst American maritime disaster, has all of the elements of tragedy and drama as does the demise of the *Titanic*, which would occur nearly a half-century later. Instead of the *Titanic's* wealthy passengers in evening clothes and immigrants, most of the *Sultana's* victims were half-starved veterans in rags. Yet the same element—the fallibility of humankind—was present in both disasters.

Put in the context of what else happened it 1865, the *Sultana* disaster was relegated deep inside major newspapers, the only media source. The Civil War had just ended, and shortly before the *Sultana* left New Orleans, President Lincoln had been assassinated. The papers were screaming about John Wilkes Booth, and there was no CNN to track down survivors of the *Sultana* to interview. One well-documented book by Civil War scholar, Gene Eric Salecker, *Disaster on the Mississippi*, details this catastrophic event.

Today, the wreckage is buried in twenty feet of mud in an Arkansas soybean field, beneath the spot where the flooded river carried her. There is no marker or memorial at the site where more than 1,500 people perished. In Memphis and Knoxville Tennessee, however, markers exist. The *Sultana* Survivors' Society, presumably the descendants of the survivors, meets yearly. Initially, nearly 800 persons were rescued, but 200 of these died after the rescue.

When Edward Kennedy recovered from his burns, he returned to Berea and took up his studies at Baldwin University. After completing his degree, he entered business, first with a drug store, then a dry goods store. He invested in a stone quarry and in real estate. Soon he became a leader in the development of the community, working with others for and investing in the Berea Street Railway. He was a founding member of the Berea Board of Trade, formed in 1903, to bring businesses to the community.

For fifty years, there were few civic undertakings in Berea in which E.J. Kennedy did not have a hand. He seemed to have an uncanny sense, perhaps some would call it a Midas touch, where investing money was concerned. He was not afraid to spend money to make money. A simple example: In his drugstore he kept a jar of stick candy, and every boy in town knew about it. One day one of his friends criticized him for handing a penny stick to a ragged-looking youngster—a sheer waste of money, said the friend.

"Oh, I don't think so," Kennedy replied. "The next time that boy's mother sends him downtown to a drug store, he'll remember that candy and come here."

Edward Kennedy, his wife Emma, and their three sons—Charles R., Edward W. and Fred L.—lived in an elegant home on Prospect Street, definitely on God's side of town. The *Advertiser* makes frequent mention of social events that took place there.

Kennedy's war record and abiding faith in the Republican Party made him an ideal candidate when he entered politics. In 1885, he was elected to the Ohio House of Representatives by a substantial margin and re-elected for a second term by an even greater margin. In Columbus, he represented interests of Berea sandstone and Berea temperance. He also represented women. A bill he introduced and championed through the legislature allowed women to vote in local elections. A few years later, Berea's Mrs. Mary Elmore was elected to the Berea school board, the first woman officeholder in the town.

In April 1888, Kennedy resigned his legislative post mid-term and ran for mayor of Berea. He was elected nearly unanimously. The *Advertiser* called this a spontaneous testimonial of the esteem in which his fellow citizens held him. In 1890, he was appointed to the State Board of Pardons by then-Governor McKinley and was reappointed by Governor Bushnell. When McKinley was elected President in 1896, Berea was a stronghold of Republican support. A rally in town on Election Eve attracted 5,000 people. When President McKinley was inaugurated the following March, the *Advertiser* noted, "Captain Kennedy and wife...are enjoying the inaugural festivities in Washington, D.C."

Kennedy made his way into county politics, serving as county recorder for a short time. Then from 1897 to 1904 he served as a Cuyahoga County Commissioner.

When real estate represented wealth, he was the town's foremost dealer, and he made a substantial fortune. Nearly every issue of the *Advertiser* in the 1890's reports the purchase of one or more pieces of property by E.J. Kennedy. Yet he definitely demonstrated a strong civic interest. "At all times," said the *Enterprise* upon his death, "he took an active part in the civic, social, and industrial welfare, and the development of the community. This is a record that few in the whole state can equal. It is a record that will live as a permanent monument to his memory."

In his last decade of public life, 1912-1922, Edward Kennedy was a founder and president of the Commercial & Savings Bank. His co-directors of the bank wrote of him in their Resolutions of Respect that "(Kennedy) was a man of courtesy and kindness who never turned away from those needing advice or assistance and whose knowledge of business laws and usages was invaluable, and whose estimate of value, whether of property or man, was almost infallible, and whose wide acquaintance and honorable reputation among the citizens of this community was a great aid in establishing this bank."

Although he had retired from the bank and civic activities two years before his death from a lung abscess, his mind was not impaired. His wife had died from peritonitis ten years earlier. Only one of their sons is buried with his parents in Woodvale Cemetery near Berea. Nearly every Berea business closed during Captain Kennedy's funeral, which was held at his Prospect Street home. His obituary does not state who conducted the service, nor does it list a church affiliation for the deceased although he is mentioned as a "leading light" in the local Masonic and Knights of Pythias lodges and the G. A. R. post.

Perhaps in the matter of church membership, Kennedy may have taken a page from Abraham Lincoln's life. When asked why he was not a member of a church (although he was a student of the Bible and took his boys to a Presbyterian church), Lincoln replied, "When I find a church that states this as a requirement for membership, that will be the church I'll join." Then he would quote Micah 6:8—"What does the Lord require of thee? To do justice, to love mercy, and to walk humbly with God."

These seem to be words that Edward J. Kennedy might have lived by—and the town of Berea became richer for that.

LaVergne, TN USA
21 March 2010
176655LV00004B/1/P